Divorce Guide
for Canada

Divorce Guide
for Canada

Alison Sawyer, BA, LLB

Self-Counsel Press
(a division of)
International Self-Counsel Press Ltd.
Canada   USA

Self-Counsel Press acknowledges the financial support of the Government of Canada through the Book Publishing Industry Development Program (BPIDP) for our publishing activities.

Printed in Canada.

First edition: 2002; Reprinted 2003

Canadian Cataloguing in Publication Data

Sawyer, Alison, 1948-
Divorce Guide for Canada

(Self-counsel legal series)
ISBN 1-55180-443-3

1. Divorce—Law and legislation—Canada—Popular works.
I. Title. II. Series
KE569.2.S28 2002   346.7101'66   C2001-911700-0
KF535.Z9S28 2002

Self-Counsel Press
(a division of)
International Self-Counsel Press Ltd.

1481 Charlotte Road	1704 N. State Street
North Vancouver, BC V7J 1H1	Bellingham, WA 98225
Canada	USA

Contents

8 Getting Started: The Basics

Acknowledgements

The author and publisher of this book would like to thank the following individuals for their valuable input in the creation of this guide.

Sandra M. Burke, LLB, of Dawe & Burke Barristers and Solicitors, St. John's, Newfoundland.

Anu Osborne, LLB, of Deely, Fabbri, Sellen, Barristers & Solicitors, Winnipeg, Manitoba.

Notice to Readers

Laws are constantly changing. Every effort is made to keep this publication as current as possible. However the author, the publisher, and the vendor of this make no representation or warranties regarding the outcome or the use to which the information in this book is put and are not assuming any liability for any claims, losses, or damages arising out of the use of this book. The reader should not rely on the author or the publisher of this book for any professional advice. Please be sure you have the most recent edition.

This book does not cover divorce law in Quebec.

Note: The fees quoted in this book are correct at the date of publication. However, fees are subject to change without notice. For current fees, please check with the court registry or appropriate government office nearest you.

Introduction

Is a do-your-own divorce right for you?

This book, written by a lawyer, is directed toward filling the public's need for information. Every person should know his or her rights and know how to use the courts to enforce these rights.

The directions and explanations contained in this book, as well as the provincial forms and instructions kits available for download from <www.self-counsel.com>, are presented in a simple step-by-step process so that anyone should be able to acquire a knowledge and understanding of divorce proceedings.

You can obtain your own divorce; it is the right of every person. You will find the process of divorce easier the more you inform yourself and become knowledgeable about this area of law. The law governing separation and divorce is complicated. This book explains all the legal terms used in the divorce forms. More important, it gives you some background in the law and court system that you need to understand in order to do your own divorce.

Doing your own divorce requires time and energy on your part, but the ultimate objective of this book and the provincial forms and instruction kits mentioned above is to make lack of money no obstacle to obtaining a divorce. Your efforts could save you hundreds of dollars in lawyer's fees. Even if you are completely unfamiliar with the operation of the law, you should be able to obtain a divorce for less than $500, provided there is no disagreement over custody or other complications.

However, there are some situations in which this book cannot help you and, in these cases, consultation with a lawyer is absolutely mandatory. Specifically, if your divorce is contested on any grounds whatsoever, you will require a lawyer. If you do not have counsel, and cannot afford a lawyer, you should consult your local legal aid office. According to past statistics, contested divorces account for only 15 percent of the total number of divorces; this book is designed for the other 85 percent.

Divorce Guide for Canada

There are two products available from Self-Counsel Press to help you obtain your own divorce: the first is this guide; the second, the provincial forms and instructions kits available for download from <www.self-counsel.com>.

The printed book contains all the information you need to know about divorce law in Canada and how the courts are structured. It contains detailed information about issues such as —

- separation agreements,

- child custody, access, and support,

- spousal support, and

- division of marital property.

It is imperative that you read through the entire book before you start to do your own divorce. If there are no children of the marriage, you do not need to read Chapter 4: Children.

Once you have read through the printed book, it's time to start preparing the paperwork for your divorce. The provincial forms and instructions kits contain —

- all the forms you will need to do your own divorce in your province or territory,

- completed samples of all the forms,

- detailed instructions for filling in each form, and

- the procedure for filing the forms in your province's or territory's court system.

The printed book and the provincial forms and instructions kits are designed to make doing your own divorce as easy as possible.

1
Divorce Law Basics

What is a divorce?

What is an annulment?

How do common-law and same-sex relationships fit in?

What if one spouse has obtained a foreign divorce?

What are the grounds for divorce?

When may a court refuse a divorce?

What is the difference between a joint divorce and a sole divorce?

Divorce Law Basics

1. What is a divorce?

A divorce is a court order dissolving the legal relationship of marriage. A court order of divorce is the only way a legal marriage can be ended. A married couple can live separate and apart for many years, but without a Divorce Order they are still legally married. Only a Divorce Order will allow either of them to remarry.

When the court makes an order for divorce, it may also include orders for spousal support and child support, access, and custody. In some provinces, you can also make property claims alongside your divorce, although division of property is not covered by the Divorce Act. You may also be able to ask the court to make an order changing the wife's and children's surnames.

2. What is an annulment?

When a marriage is annulled, a judge declares that there was no legal marriage in the first place. A number of circumstances can be the basis for an annulment.

Definition: Divorce

A decision of a judge (in the form of an order or judgment) ending a marriage. The order is made under the authority given the court by the federal Divorce Act.

It's the law

The annulment discussed in this book is obtained through the courts under civil law. Annulment under the rules of a particular religion does not affect the legal status of a marriage.

2.1 Bigamy

There is no legal marriage when one person in the marriage is legally married to someone else at the time of the marriage. It doesn't matter where the first marriage took place or if it was under the laws of another country. The second marriage is called a bigamous marriage and can be annulled.

2.2 Lack of capacity

A marriage might be annulled when one person in the marriage lacks the legal capacity to marry. One example of lack of capacity is when one person is under the legal age of marriage and his or her guardian has not agreed to the marriage. Other examples include circumstances in which one person is not mentally able to understand the concept of marriage or the parties are too closely related. Your provincial department responsible for issuing marriage licences can provide more information on these rules.

2.3 Failure to consummate the marriage

The most talked about reason for annulment is sexual impotence or failure to consummate the marriage. Legally, for the purposes of annulment, one of the parties must have a physical, mental, or emotional inability to have sexual intercourse. This inability must have been in existence at the time of the marriage ceremony.

2.4 Lack of consent

The most difficult circumstance to establish as a reason for an annulment is one in which there has been a lack of consent to the marriage by reason of duress, fear, or fraud.

If someone was induced to enter into the contract of marriage by threats of personal violence, the court might consider annulling the marriage because the person was not able to enter into the contract of his or her own free will, but was doing so under duress.

Fraud is determined by establishing whether the parties to the marriage understood that they were going through a ceremony of marriage. Cases in which one person was paid to enter into a marriage to help another person gain landed immigrant status are clearly not fraud unless the person being paid did not understand that he or she was entering into a legal marriage.

Annulment is a complex area of the law. If you suspect that your circumstances might establish a ground for annulment, consult a lawyer. It is not an area of the law that can be pursued without legal advice and representation.

3. How do common-law and same-sex relationships fit in?

Only people who are legally married can get divorced under the Divorce Act. The federal government has the legislative authority to make law regarding marriage and divorce, although the Divorce Act (which is a federal act) does not give a definition of marriage. The responsibility for making laws about the procedures for getting married is provincial.

While the provincial marriage statutes do not define marriage, they set out the legal requirements that have to be met in order to register the marriage. According to the law of most Canadian provinces and territories, to be legally married, two people must have gone through either a religious or a civil ceremony in the presence of each other and at least two witnesses. Usually, the marriage is proved by providing proof of registration of the marriage with a government body (i.e., a provincial department of vital statistics).

The provincial legislation covering family law (i.e., marital property, custody, and support) does define the concept of a spouse, and provincial legislation on family law issues uses the word "spouse" or "spouses" rather than "married."

Traditionally, spouses have been defined as "a man and a woman living together in a conjugal relationship" or "a person married to a person of the opposite sex." In 2000, the Supreme Court of Canada ruled that these definitions of spouse are discriminatory for the purposes of provincial legislation dealing with such matters as support and benefits, and are contrary to the Charter of Rights and Freedoms. Parliament passed the Modernization of Benefits and Obligations Act in response to

Tip

For a definition of marriage, Canadian law at both the federal and provincial level has relied on the common law (or judge-made law) that we brought into our law from England.

Definition: Spouse

One of two people who live in a marriage-like relationship, meaning the people co-habit and have a sexual component to the relationship. Traditionally, this has been defined as a man and a woman, but now most provinces and territories include common-law and same-sex relationships in the definition of spouse.

this ruling. The act amends a large number of acts with regard to the meaning of "spouse."

As a result, provincial legislators have changed the definition of spouse to include common-law and same-sex relationships, usually with the proviso that the two people have lived together for anywhere from one year to three years. (The definition varies from province to province, from territory to territory, and from one piece of legislation to another. Not all provinces and territories have changed the definition of spouse, but they do all extend legislation to include same-sex partners.)

It's the law

The Divorce Act does not apply to unmarried people. The provinces and territories have exclusive authority to make law governing the affairs of unmarried couples and their children (common-law or same-sex partners and single parents).

The definition of marriage may soon become the subject of scrutiny by the Supreme Court of Canada. Until then, in accordance with provincial marriage law, only a heterosexual couple can get married. Therefore only a heterosexual couple can get divorced under the Divorce Act.

It's the law

"...the amendments made by this Act do not affect the meaning of the word 'marriage,' that is, the lawful union of one man and one woman to the exclusion of all others."

MODERNIZATION OF BENEFITS AND OBLIGATIONS ACT,
S.C. 2000, C. 12, SECTION 1.

4. What if one spouse has obtained a foreign divorce?

A divorce obtained in a country other than Canada is a valid and effective divorce in Canada as long as one of the spouses had a "real and substantial connection" with the country granting the divorce.

The Canadian Divorce Act requires that the person getting the foreign divorce has been "ordinarily resident" in the country granting the divorce. This means that the foreign country has been his or her place of usual residence for at least one year immediately before starting the divorce proceedings.

If that requirement is not met, then Canadian law does not recognize the foreign divorce and considers the spouses to be legally married. Neither one of the spouses can get remarried in Canada.

It's the law

In some provinces or territories, you may be required to get a lawyer's opinion on the validity of your foreign divorce in order to get a licence for remarriage.

Definition: Superior Court
The higher court in the province or territory that falls between the provincial court and the court of appeal. Some provinces call it Supreme Court, as in the Supreme Court of British Columbia. Other provinces call it Queen's Bench, as in the Court of Queen's Bench. These courts can hear family and divorce applications.

5. What are the grounds for divorce?

The Divorce Act allows for only one ground for divorce: there has to be a breakdown of the marriage. A breakdown of marriage can only be established under one of the following three situations:

- Living separate and apart for more than one year

- Adultery

- Cruelty

It's the law

8.(2) Breakdown of a marriage is established only if:

(a) the spouses have lived separate and apart for at least one year immediately preceding the determination of the divorce proceeding and were living separate and apart at the commencement of the proceeding; or

(b) the spouse against whom the divorce proceeding is brought has, since celebration of the marriage,

(i) committed adultery, or

(ii) treated the other spouse with physical or mental cruelty of such a kind as to render intolerable the continued cohabitation of the spouses.

SECTION 8(2) DIVORCE ACT R.S., 1985,
C. 3 (2ND SUPP.)SBE

5.1 Separation for more than one year

The simplest ground for divorce is living separate and apart for more than one year immediately before the granting of the divorce. This is sometimes referred to as "no fault" divorce, because fault is not an issue, and either you or your spouse or both of you together may proceed under this section.

It is the simplest reason to give for divorce because all you must prove is that —

- you and your spouse were physically separated for one year, and

- it was the intention of either the husband or the wife that there be physical separation. (The court will usually accept the statement of the applicant in this regard without requiring additional proof.)

There have been cases of people getting divorced on this ground even though they lived at the same address for the one-year period. You can live in the same house as your spouse if you conducted your life completely separately, although it is much easier to prove this ground if you can say that one person lived in separately locked and inaccessible living quarters.

Tip

If you are using separation for more than one year as grounds for a divorce, you can have continued to have sexual relations with your spouse throughout the one-year period, but you cannot have actually resided together for more than 90 days.

The Divorce Act allows for attempts at reconciliation. Both spouses must have the desire to reconcile and can reside together for a period (in total during the one-year period) of less than 90 days. If you reside together for more than 90 days, you cannot use separation for one year as a ground for divorce unless you start counting the one-year period from when you ceased cohabitating the second time.

5.2 Adultery or cruelty

If you are using adultery or cruelty as a ground for divorce, you must be able to prove that your spouse has either committed adultery or has treated you with physical or mental cruelty that has made it impossible for you to continue living together. You cannot use these grounds merely to make a point to your spouse.

Adultery or cruelty can often be difficult to prove. They are not recommended if you are doing your own divorce, for the following reasons:

- Some provinces require a court appearance where you give oral testimony and have a witness to corroborate the grounds if one of these grounds is used as the reason for marital breakdown.

- Often, when adultery or cruelty is used as a ground for divorce, the respondent (the spouse being accused of committing adultery or cruelty) will contest the divorce and file a response.

- These grounds are more complicated to prove to the satisfaction of the judge (even if the respondent has not contested the application).

When your spouse is not going to contest the divorce, it would be much easier to do the divorce without a lawyer on the one-year separation ground than to use adultery or cruelty as a ground for divorce. If you want to use adultery or cruelty, it is recommended that you consult a lawyer.

If you use adultery or cruelty as a ground for divorce, you don't have to wait the one-year separation period before finalizing your divorce. However, you must have separated immediately after the adultery was discovered or an act of cruelty happened. The adultery can have occurred after the parties have separated.

Definition: Reconciliation
When the married couple who have separated move back in together in an effort to settle their differences and to make the marriage work. Under the Divorce Act, the period of living together for this purpose has to be less than 90 days of the one-year period immediately preceding the Order for Divorce.

Tip
You can start your divorce action before the one-year period has expired. However, the one-year separation period must have expired before the final grant of divorce is made.

Tip

The defendant is known as the respondent in some provinces and territories. The plaintiff is known as the petitioner or applicant in some provinces and territories.

Tip

The person making the application for divorce cannot be the one who committed the adultery or cruelty.

The Divorce Act explicitly states that in making an order for spousal support, the judge is not to allow any misconduct (i.e., adultery or cruelty) to influence his or her decision. In making an order for custody or access, the judge may only consider conduct that is directly related to the parties' abilities to act as parents to the child. In other words, it is only in some family circumstances that using adultery or cruelty as a ground for divorce will matter to the issue of custody and access.

You must provide proof of the adultery or cruelty in a form acceptable to the court — usually a sworn statement of admission by the offending spouse or the third party (the one with whom adultery was committed). In the case of cruelty, you will need a sworn statement by someone who can corroborate the cruelty (e.g., a medical doctor or counsellor). The cruelty has to be fairly extreme or excessive in the eyes of the person offended. It also has to be a course of conduct and not just one act of cruelty, unless the act was exceptional. Adultery, however, can be based on one incident.

If the evidence is not prepared and presented in the proper form, the court will likely ask you and your spouse to appear in person to explain the adultery or cruelty. The third party to the adultery or a witness to the adultery or cruelty may also have to appear. The judge has to be satisfied that it is more likely than not that there was cruelty or adultery. In some provinces and territories, if you use one of these grounds you have no choice but to appear at an oral hearing in front of a judge, in addition to filing an affidavit from someone corroborating your evidence.

The judge also has to find that the adultery really happened and was not made up. In other words, the judge has to be satisfied that there was no agreement between the parties to manufacture evidence or agree upon the evidence used to establish the ground for divorce (this is called collusion and is discussed in the next section).

6. When may a court refuse a divorce?

They are four reasons why the court may refuse a divorce. The first is the most common. The other three are rare. Your application for divorce will not be refused if your spouse wants to stay married or if your spouse objects for religious reasons. Only the reasons listed below lead to refusal.

6.1 No child support

The court has a legal duty to inquire into whether or not satisfactory child support has been arranged. Since 1997, the federal government has legislated the amount of child support that must be paid according to the non-custodial parent's income. The amount can be different (less) if it can be shown that it would cause a spouse undue hardship to have to pay the guideline amount. Or it can be a higher amount if it can be shown that the child's upbringing requires special expenses.

Parents cannot agree between them that child support is not going to be paid unless there are unusual circumstances. The court will refuse the application for divorce if what it considers reasonable arrangements have not been agreed upon by both spouses. If there is no arrangement, the court will order the guideline amount to be paid. See Chapter 4 for more information on child support.

6.2 Collusion

Collusion occurs when people conspire to lie to the court or make up or hide evidence for the purpose of deceiving the court. For example, you and your spouse cannot conspire to make up a ground for divorce. You have either been living separate and apart for one year or you have not. Your spouse either committed adultery or he or she did not.

Collusion must involve deception. It is not a conspiracy to deceive if your spouse tells you about his or her adultery and provides you with evidence to support your application for divorce.

6.3 Condonation

In divorce law, condonation means forgiveness of any act or acts being used as grounds for divorce. It does not apply where the ground for divorce is living separate and apart for one year. In practical terms, if you continued to live with your spouse or returned to live with your spouse after learning of an act of adultery or after an act of cruelty, you have condoned the act.

However, the Divorce Act encourages attempts at reconciliation. If you left your spouse immediately after he or she committed an act of adultery or cruelty, started the divorce, and then

Definition: Hearing
A court proceeding where one or both parties appear in front of the judge or other court official (e.g., registrar or master) assigned to their case. The proceeding may be a trial or it may be a procedural application. The judge, registrar, or master hears the evidence, which is presented either in the form of affidavits or sworn oral testimony. The parties also make oral argument to convince the judge to make a decision that will favour one side or the other.

Definition: Court
Refers to the court house, the building housing the court rooms, the judge's chambers (offices), and the court registry. The word is also an impersonal and powerful way of referring to the judge, as in "this court orders..." or "the court decided...."

Tip

If you don't show that an arrangement for child support has been made and agreed upon in your application for divorce, the court will order that the federal guideline amount be paid.

Tip

A separation agreement (if done properly) is a legal and binding agreement, and is not considered to be collusion.

Tip

All the provinces and territories have procedures for joint petitions for divorce except Alberta and Newfoundland and Labrador. Alberta is intending to change their rules to allow joint divorces, so check with your local court registry before proceeding.

attempted unsuccessfully to reconcile, the court has the discretion to grant the divorce.

6.4 Connivance

If you actively encourage your spouse to commit adultery or stand idly by and don't object, you cannot then start a divorce on the grounds that your spouse committed adultery. This is known as connivance. The court will only grant the divorce if it can be shown that there was no active encouragement of the adultery.

7. What is the difference between a joint divorce and a sole divorce?

Before you start divorce proceedings, you will need to decide whether you are going to file for a joint divorce or a sole divorce. In a joint divorce, both spouses file jointly for the divorce. In a sole divorce, one spouse files for divorce and the other spouse responds.

A joint divorce is usually easier to do than a sole divorce because both spouses agree to the contents of the divorce. In most provinces and territories that allow for joint divorces, you can only use the ground of living separate and apart for one year for this type of divorce. A joint divorce is not recommended where the parties do not live close to each other and are not on good speaking terms. In a joint divorce, both spouses have to sign the court documents starting the divorce action. Then, after filing and waiting, both have to sign affidavits dated at that time. See Chapter 8 for more information on filing for a joint or sole divorce.

If you do not want to have any contact with your spouse, you may wish to consider a sole divorce. In an undefended divorce started by just one person, the other spouse does nothing except receive a copy of the original court documents. However, a sole divorce can cost more because your spouse has to be served the court documents. See Chapter 8 for more information on service.

2
The Power of the Courts

What laws can the provinces and territories make?

Should I proceed under provincial or federal legislation?

Are the divorce procedures the same in each province and territory?

What can the courts order before I get divorced?

The Power of the Courts

The Constitution Act of Canada gives the federal government the power to make laws regarding marriage and divorce. The federal Divorce Act is the written legislation that lays out the law of divorce, as well as rules about related issues that people often cover in their Divorce Order, such as —

- child custody, access, and support, and

- spousal support.

Because the Divorce Act is federal legislation, any judgments or court orders made under it overrule orders on the same matters made under provincial legislation. The orders made under the Divorce Act are enforceable anywhere in Canada by any federal or provincial court.

It's the law

The Divorce Act was passed in its present form in 1985 and amended in 1997. The federal government is currently studying proposals to amend the Divorce Act again, possibly in the year 2002 or 2003.

The 1997 amendments dealt primarily with child support. If the government decides to proceed with the proposals now being formulated, the upcoming amendments will concern child custody and access.

Tip

Marital property may also be called family assets, matrimonial property, or property used for a family purpose, depending on which province or territory you are in. For more information on marital property, see Chapter 6.

Definition: Affidavit divorce

An affidavit divorce is an uncontested divorce in which the other spouse does not file a Statement of Defense or Answer and the parties do not attend at the court to appear before a judge. An affidavit divorce is recommended if you will be preparing and filing the divorce application without a lawyer. In some provinces and territories it is known as a desk-order or desk divorce. **Note:** In some provinces, you will need to appear in court even if the divorce is uncontested.

1. What laws can the provinces and territories make?

The Constitution Act gives the provinces and territories authority to make laws concerning property and civil rights. This power gives the provinces and territories much broader scope than the federal government has with regard to family law matters.

All the provincial governments have passed legislation covering the following family law matters:

- Child custody and access

- Guardianship

- Spousal support and child support

- Adoption

- Matrimonial property (or family assets) and division of property after separation

- Succession (wills and probate/administration of estates)

- Names

The provinces and territories and the federal government share their authority with regards to separating and divorcing married couples and making orders to do with child custody, access, and support and spousal support. However, only provincial law covers division of matrimonial property. Provincial law also has authority over the court procedure for administering the Divorce Act.

2. Should I proceed under provincial or federal legislation?

If you are married, you can choose whether to deal with issues of custody, access, and support under provincial family law or under the federal Divorce Act. If you have already separated from your spouse and are not ready or willing to start divorce proceedings but need to deal with property, finances, and children, you can start your legal actions under provincial legislation. When you are ready to divorce, you will have to start your divorce action under the federal Divorce Act. You can include any of the above matters in the application for divorce even if you already have a court order under provincial law for child custody, access, or support or spousal support. The divorce proceedings then supersede the provincial court matters.

When you are ready to divorce, you can choose to —

- deal with child custody, access, and support under the Divorce Act, or

- deal with all the above matters plus the division of marital property under provincial legislation, but included in the divorce application (although you will probably not be able to proceed without a lawyer), or

- not deal with any of these matters (e.g., if you have included them in your separation agreement or already have court orders and don't want to make them part of your divorce proceedings).

Remember, if you haven't dealt with division of family assets, you may lose your entitlement to the assets under some provincial laws once the divorce is granted, or very shortly thereafter. You should consult a lawyer before beginning your application for divorce.

In some cases, there are advantages to proceeding under provincial legislation separately from divorce proceedings. Some provinces have a lower court, called Provincial Court, which can deal with family and child issues. Other provinces have a Unified Family Court for all family and child matters. These courts are often more user friendly than the Supreme Court. The forms and court procedures are simpler and there is often a staff service to assist people who do not have lawyers.

Another advantage of using provincial legislation is that if your spouse is agreeable and you have the help of the family court service, you can more easily get orders by consent before applying for divorce than if you applied under the federal Divorce Act. (See Section **4.** for more information on orders by consent.)

Deciding whether to use provincial family legislation or the federal divorce law is a difficult question in family law. If you cannot afford a lawyer or get legal aid, and you do not have an

Tip
See Chapter 7 for more information on doing an affidavit divorce.

Tip
If you want to vary a custody, access, and support order you must apply to the same court (i.e., Provincial or Superior) that made the initial order. Variation of orders is tricky. Check with your local family court services or with a lawyer.

Definition: Civil procedure
Each provincial government has legislation that sets out the court system in its province or territory. Part of the legislation are regulations called the Rules of Court, which have to be followed for all legal proceedings.

Tip

If you have matters that are in dispute, they must be settled before applying for an affidavit divorce.

Tip

The staff at your local family court will be able to tell you if they have any or all of the following services:

- Information and referral service
- Legal aid for family matters
- Mediation service
- Seminars on parenting after separation

To find your nearest family court, look in the Blue Pages under any of the following: Courts, Court Services, Family Information/ Family Justice Centres, Legal Aid, Department of Justice, or Attorney General. You can also go to <http://canada.justice.gc.ca/en/ps/cca/invent/main.htm>.

agreement with your spouse, it is probably easier to use provincial law. You cannot apply for an affidavit divorce in most provinces and territories if you are also asking for orders regarding matters in dispute. All matters other than divorce have to be by consent or agreement when you apply for an affidavit divorce.

3. Are the divorce procedures the same in each province and territory?

The Constitution Act gives the provinces and territories responsibility for the administration of their court systems and for the rules of civil procedure. Each province and territory, therefore, has its own court rules that set out the court forms and procedures that must be followed for applications under all the different laws, whether provincial or federal. For this reason, the actual paperwork and court registry procedures for applying for divorce under the federal Divorce Act vary from province to province and from territory to territory. The step-by-step instructions included in the provincial forms and instructions kits available for download from <www.self-counsel.com> lead you through the court rules for your province or territory.

The Rules of Court set out all aspects of the procedures that must be followed in the courts — from the type and form of all court documents to notice requirements, fees, and types of proceedings that may be brought in the different courts.

4. What can the courts order before I get divorced?

The courts have power to grant more than just Divorce Orders. When separation occurs, it is often immediately necessary to stabilize the family situation. One spouse may be threatening to take the children far away so that the other spouse will not be able to see them. The departing spouse may have left with no word about how his or her income will be replaced. Creditors might be ready to take action. If there is no agreement in place between the separating spouses and no indication of any intention to deal with these issues, then you may want to apply to the court for a court order before you start divorce proceedings. You cannot proceed with an affidavit divorce until the contested matters have been finalized.

4.1 Consent orders

Many family courts have counsellors who can advise you on how to take action in that court. Some counsellors will attempt to contact your spouse to try to mediate or negotiate an agreement.

If successful, the counsellor will then draft a consent order for each spouse to sign. The signed draft will be signed by a judge without either one of the spouses needing to appear in person. The order is just as binding as if obtained after a hearing.

If either your circumstances or your spouse's circumstances change, you can apply to the court to vary the consent order.

4.2 Disputed matters

If you and your spouse are not able to agree on financial, property, or child-related matters before you start your divorce, then either one of you can make an application for court orders dealing with the disputed issues to family court.

For people needing to make application to settle disputed matters, family courts have simple application forms designed to be completed by people not represented by lawyers. The application has to be filled in, filed at the court registry, and served on your spouse. Your spouse may choose to file a response indicating that he or she is disputing the application. If there is a dispute, the case has to be set down for hearing. The word hearing includes trial. Contact your family court services for more information on how to proceed. If you want to apply for spousal support or a division of property, it would be a good idea to see a lawyer.

Most family courts have lengthy waiting lists, so the hearing might not take place for several months. If your situation is urgent, you can apply for a temporary order (also called interim order). You and your spouse (if he or she is disputing your application) will have to appear in front of a judge for a mini hearing. After hearing from both sides (or just one side if the other spouse doesn't come), the judge will make temporary orders to deal with children and support until the case can be fully aired at a trial.

Definition: Affidavit

An affidavit is a numbered set of statements of facts, written in your own words, that you know to be true. The affidavit must be signed before a commissioner for oaths, a notary public, or a lawyer. That person will ask you to swear an oath or affirm that the information given in the affidavit is true to the best of your knowledge. It is a crime to swear an affidavit that contains false statements. The affidavit can be used in any court proceeding as evidence that the facts set out in it are believed or known to be true by the person who has sworn the affidavit.

Tip

Some provinces and territories allow you to apply to vary a Divorce Order or other Superior Court order in provincial court. Check with your court staff.

4.3 Varying or enforcing a court order

Many couples negotiate and sign a separation agreement that lays out the terms of their separation before they get divorced (see Chapter 3). If your spouse is not living up to the terms of your separation agreement or a consent court order, you may need to make an interim application for a court order to enforce the agreement or court order. All provinces and territories have a court service to assist with obtaining child support and for enforcing support orders. However, most court services do not help with enforcing agreements involving marital property or child custody and access. For that, particularly where property or spousal support is involved, you should have the help of a lawyer. Legal aid may provide assistance in your province or territory.

If you have started an action under the provincial family legislation or under the Divorce Act, you can obtain interim or temporary orders in the family court.

If you got an order in family court and need to enforce or vary it, apply to that court. However, if you have started a divorce action and want a temporary (interim) order, you should apply to the court where you filed your application for divorce.

A variation or enforcement proceeding in superior court will be heard in chambers, which is a small courtroom designed for applications that are not trials. You will have to provide evidence by filing sworn written statements called affidavits.

The order obtained in the interim hearing is not necessarily the same as the order that will be obtained after a trial. However, in the case of children, the court often prefers to maintain the status quo.

It is preferable to be represented by a lawyer for applications to family court when it is a division of the Superior Court of your province or territory, but more and more people are going to the Superior Court without counsel. If you choose to represent yourself in family court, remember that attempting to present a case yourself is difficult and time consuming. The court registry will not accept documents unless they are in the proper form, and because of the increasing number of unrepresented litigants, registry staff may not be as helpful as they once were. See Chapter 7 for more information about hiring a lawyer.

3
Marriage and Separation Agreements

What are marriage agreements and domestic contracts?

What are separation agreements?

Marriage and Separation Agreements

1. What are marriage agreements and domestic contracts?

Some couples sign a written contract either before they are married (i.e., a pre-nuptial agreement) or after they are married (i.e., a marriage agreement). In some provinces and territories these are referred to as domestic contracts. These contracts typically set out what property or assets each person is bringing into the marriage, and specify who will get ownership of the property and assets at the time of separation or divorce. Some agreements also deal with issues related to the children of a marriage.

A domestic contract cannot dictate the terms of the actual divorce itself. The terms can be incorporated into a Divorce Order and, if stated in the agreement, can continue to apply after the divorce. They can also be varied at the time of divorce if the parties agree to include the new terms in the application for divorce.

2. What are separation agreements?

Once a couple is living separate and apart, they don't have to do anything to make the separation legal. Nor is there a law that compels a couple to take any legal action to separate their affairs.

Some couples do nothing to legally clarify their situation after separation. If they don't, they may find they are still financially responsible for each other in some way, or a school or hospital might question the right of one parent to custody of the children.

Many couples are willing to work out an agreement, but not everyone actually signs a written separation agreement. Where

Tip
A marriage agreement is written before separation, while a separation agreement is written after separation. Both agreements are intended to bind the parties at the time of separation with respect to the division of property and, sometimes, with respect to custody of children.

children are involved and there is no agreement or even understanding of what the spouses are planning to do long term, then it is appropriate for the custodial parent to get a court order outlining the terms of the separation. Without a court order or separation agreement, the non-custodial parent may simply come back and take the children away. This also applies to marital property. If it was property used for a family purpose, both parties are entitled to share in it. The only way to make the agreed upon terms and arrangements enforceable is by a written and signed separation agreement in accordance with the law of your province or territory, or by court order.

If there is a court order for custody, the court may have ordered that both parents have custody, with primary residence of the child being with one parent. If there is no court order or agreement, both parents have the right to custody, but the parent with whom the child lives is in fact the custodial parent.

2.1 Verbal separation agreements

Some separating couples put nothing in writing because they have come to a verbal understanding. Often, spouses do not see the need for a written agreement when there is little in the way of marital property and/or no children.

A verbal understanding is fine if not much can go wrong. For example, if the only marital property is household goods, a car, and credit card debt, these items can be easily divided. As long as each spouse follows through with the paperwork to put the understanding into effect, the consequences of not having a written agreement may be small.

However, a verbal agreement may not be enforceable when things do go wrong, such as if one spouse lies or has a different understanding of the terms. If your spouse agreed to transfer the car registration and insurance into his or her name but didn't, then you can become liable when that wasn't the intention. A verbal agreement will not matter to your insurance agency. If you co-signed or guaranteed a loan for your spouse, then you can be made responsible for the debt if your spouse defaults. The fact that you are separated will not matter to the bank because you both signed the loan document, and each agreed separately to be responsible for the debt of the other. Until the principal borrower and the bank come to a new agreement, that loan document will continue to be enforceable against both of you despite the separation.

Sometimes, when spouses separate without a written agreement, some consequences of separating are overlooked. One spouse may be willing to go along with whatever the other wants at the time. Potentially controversial issues are then not dealt with. For example, the pressure to separate might be so strong that financial considerations seem of little importance. Spousal support is therefore not discussed, even though one spouse earns considerably more than the other. Or an RRSP might not be divided because neither spouse thought of it as marital property. Years might pass with these matters not being considered, and then when emotions have calmed and one spouse's financial situation becomes desperate, the time limitation for dealing with marital property is up. The best solution is to put your separation agreement in writing.

2.2 Written separation agreements

A written separation agreement, if properly executed, is a legal contract. The contract sets out the rights and obligations of each spouse after separation. It may include clauses such as, "neither party shall harass the other," as well as the arrangements agreed upon, such as, "the non-custodial parent shall have reasonable and generous access to the children of the marriage upon the giving of two days' notice by telephone message."

A separation agreement may include the following matters:

- Custody of children

- Guardianship of children

- Access and support of children

- Title and possession of all marital property (family assets) such as the home, family business, pensions, and RRSPs

- Spousal support

2.3 Negotiation of a separation agreement

You and your spouse may wish to start negotiating your separation agreement by writing down what each of you wants and what you would like to see happen. You should cover how the

Tip

See Chapter 6 for more information on time limitations for property claims.

Definition: Executed

To execute a contract means to complete a contract in proper form. For a separation agreement to be legal, it must be dated, signed, witnessed, and, in some provinces and territories, a certificate of independent legal advice must be affixed.

household goods and family property are going to be divided and what arrangements are going to be made so that the members of the family are able to survive economically. As a way to support the fairness of the agreement, most provinces and territories have an explicit obligation for financial disclosure by both spouses.

A separation agreement can be negotiated before a couple actually physically separates from each other. However, it cannot be signed until after the separation has actually happened.

One of the premises that is fundamental to successful negotiation of a separation agreement is that both parties are negotiating honestly and in good faith. This means that nothing is hidden or kept from the discussions.

It's the law

Both spouses are legally required to disclose all their financial information to their spouse when drawing up a separation agreement or filing for divorce.

The negotiation process can take many months. As part of the obligation for financial disclosure, the spouses should ensure that they are each kept updated on changes to the original financial disclosure.

If the relationship is too strained for you and your spouse to negotiate a settlement, then a trained mediator, counsellor, or lawyer can facilitate the negotiation process. If one spouse has a lawyer draft an agreement, then the other spouse must be given ample opportunity to review the document and seek independent legal advice before signing it (see the section below).

2.4 What is the effect of a written separation agreement?

The family law in each province and territory usually sets out the requirements for separation agreements to be legally enforceable in court. At a minimum, there should be one independent witness for each signature and written disclosure of

Tip

If a separation agreement does not meet the requirements set out in the provincial family law, the court may still consider the document to be a contract setting out the intentions of the parties, and may uphold its intentions.

financial information when the agreement is dealing with property or money matters.

Some provinces and territories require that there be a certificate of independent legal advice from two different lawyers — one for each spouse. Done in this way, if the terms are not kept, the agreement can be filed in court and the court can be used to enforce it as if it were a court order. The terms of a legally drafted and signed separation agreement can also be incorporated into a Divorce Order.

The best way to ensure that a separation agreement is binding and enforceable is by going to see a lawyer either for review of the agreement you have drafted or for the lawyer to draft one for your particular situation. A lawyer will ensure that all the legal requirements are satisfied. Problems with separation agreements most often arise when one spouse is in a stronger bargaining position than the other, or when one spouse has a lawyer and the other signs without receiving independent legal advice. This can be easily avoided if both spouses consult a lawyer.

2.5 Can a separation agreement be set aside or varied?

Separation agreements need to be negotiated and entered into fairly with both parties fully informed of all the circumstances of each party and fully informed of their legal rights and obligations. If an agreement is too one-sided, it may be challenged by application to a court.

The family law legislation of each province and territory allows for the spouses to enter into a valid, enforceable contract, but sets out the circumstances that allow the court to override the terms of the agreement. In some provinces and territories, the family legislation sets out that "unfairness" is the trigger; in others, it is if one spouse turns to public assistance for support. In addition, regardless of the provincial legislation, contracts can always be challenged if there was procedural unfairness in the negotiating of the agreement, as set out below.

All terms of an agreement can be varied by the parties as long as both parties are in agreement to the change. The change must be put in writing and signed by both parties just as the original agreement was. However, it can often be difficult to get

Tip
The court will check the separation agreement to ensure that both parties have had legal advice, have fully disclosed their financial circumstances, and have otherwise met the legal requirements for a separation agreement.

Tip

The terms of a separation agreement can be changed even if they are incorporated into a court order, such as a Divorce Order, and even if the agreement was made years ago.

agreement on just one item without changing other terms because the agreement reflects a give and take between the parties. While the courts' stated preference is to give a great deal of weight to negotiated agreements, they are prepared to set them aside or modify the terms if one spouse is suffering severe economic consequences arising from a change of circumstances.

The arrangements with respect to children can always be varied if a court finds they are not in the best interests of the child, or if the child support arrangements (or lack of them) are unreasonable. They can also be varied when there is a change of circumstances, regardless of any agreement between the parents.

In addition to the considerations discussed above regarding unfairness, an agreement will be set aside by a court, which means that the terms will be changed, for any of the following reasons:

- **Duress:** This is where one spouse pressures the other into signing. The agreement will not likely be considered to be a valid contract if it was signed when emotions were running high — for example, if it was signed in the living room on the day of separation having been drafted by spouse's lawyer without the other spouse having an opportunity to review it privately.

- **Material misrepresentation:** If the financial or property information is not complete or current, or is false or misleading, the agreement can be set aside.

- **Unconscionability:** If the terms of the agreement are so harsh as to be unjust as a result of the one party knowing that the other party was in a vulnerable state and taking advantage of that knowledge to extract a grossly unfair bargain, the agreement can be set aside.

- **Undue influence:** The agreement will not be valid where one party holds out inducements such as "allowing" the other to have sole custody of the children in exchange for clear title to his or her half of the matrimonial home.

For more information on separation agreements, see *Separation Agreement*, another title in the Self-Counsel Legal Series.

4
Children

What are parental rights and responsibilities?

Who gets custody?

How do we arrange access?

How is child support determined?

Children

There is more to ending the legal relationship of marriage than obtaining the actual Order for Divorce. Children, property, and financial needs are all issues that need to be solved when a relationship ends. If these issues have not been addressed in a separation agreement or consent court order, and one of the spouses wants to get divorced, then your application for divorce should include the outstanding issues. Remember though, that you won't be able to do an affidavit divorce unless your spouse is willing to show agreement with what you ask for in your divorce, either by signing a separation agreement or consent order or by not contesting the divorce.

The next three chapters introduce you to some issues you should consider regarding children, spousal support, and family assets.

1. What are parental rights and responsibilities?

An order to do with children, whether it concerns custody, access, or support, can always be varied. The original order may have been made under the provincial laws governing families and children, or under the Divorce Act. Either parent can apply to the court to change the terms of the order if there has been a change of circumstances. The arrangements regarding the children could be in a separation agreement. It, too, can be changed if both parents can agree. If they can't, a judge can order different arrangements in accordance with parental rights and responsibilities. These rights and responsibilities are set out below.

1.1 Who is a child of a marriage?

The Divorce Act allows spouses to request custody, access, and support orders of the court for children of the marriage. A child

Definition: Child of the marriage

Any child to whom the spouses act as parents. This includes children who are not biologically related to the spouses, such as step-children and children who are adopted.

Definition: Parental charge

When a child is under parental charge, it means that the adult child is still accepting direction from the custodial parent.

of a marriage is a child of the two spouses who is under the age of majority (see below). The child must be dependent on his or her parents for support and under parental charge at the time the court makes its order.

A court order for custody, access, and support can be effective after a child is over the age of majority if he or she is still dependent and under parental charge. Examples are when he or she has a disability or is living at home, attending school, college, or university, and is financially dependent on his or her parents.

1.2 What is the age of majority?

The age of majority is the age at which a child becomes an adult with the right to enter into legally binding contracts. The age is 18 in some provinces and 19 in other provinces and territories.

The age of majority is 18 in:

- Alberta
- Manitoba
- Ontario
- Quebec
- Prince Edward Island
- Saskatchewan

The age of majority is 19 in:

- British Columbia
- New Brunswick
- Newfoundland and Labrador
- Northwest Territories
- Nova Scotia
- Nunavut
- Yukon

The age at which various laws apply to young people varies as well. For example, the Young Offenders Act doesn't apply to youths once they reach the age of 18. It is a criminal offence not to provide the necessaries of life to a young person up to the age of 16. Child support is payable until the child of a marriage reaches the age of majority for that province or territory or until he or she is no longer dependent or under parental charge.

1.3 Can someone other than a parent claim custody and access rights?

Under provincial legislation and under the Divorce Act, a person other than the biological parents may claim a right to custody and/or access of a child, including —

- grandparents,
- other relatives,
- step-parents who have not legally adopted the child, and
- same-sex partners.

Generally, that person must have a sufficient interest in or connection established with the child and an intention to treat the child as a member of his or her family. That person is then also responsible for the payment of child support if he or she separates from the family.

2. Who gets custody?

The first thing that separating parents (or the courts) must decide is who will have custody of the child of the marriage (i.e., where the child's primary residence will be). The custodial parent has primary responsibility for the child's welfare and well-being, and has care and control of the child.

> **It's the law**
>
> "...custody includes care, upbringing and any other incident of custody."
>
> *Divorce Act*, Section 2(1),
> R.S., 1985, C. 3 (2nd Supp.)

2.1 Joint versus sole custody

At the time of separation, each biological parent has equal right to custody of the children.

In the past, the courts tended to grant sole custody to one parent. That parent would have the right to make all the decisions concerning the care of the children by himself or herself. Today, the courts are making more and more decisions giving both parents equal rights to share in the decision-making, and joint custody is more common. Some parents may decide on their own to try a joint custody arrangement. Both parents are then equally responsible for making the decisions about how the children will be raised.

Joint custody can work in two different ways:

- The child could have primary residency with one parent, with the other parent seeing the child on weekends and holidays. Both parents share in all the decision-making.

- The child could spend an equal amount of time with each parent — for example, by spending every other week with each parent, or three and a half days with one then three and a half days with the other, or by switching residences every month.

Joint custody will only work when both parents are co-operative and available for a continuous exchange of information about the child. It will not work if they are antagonistic and have difficulty communicating, or if the parents are not willing to rise above their differences for the sake of their child.

It's the law

If a child spends at least 40 percent of the time with each parent, child support is not payable in accordance with the Guideline table amount, although the courts will order some amount be paid in accordance with needs, means, and circumstances. See more on child support later in this chapter for more information.

2.2 Guardianship

It is often difficult to separate custody issues from guardianship issues. The custodial parent is responsible for the day-to-day decision-making of how to raise the child. The guardian, however, is responsible for any major decisions concerning a child's welfare, including the following:

- What religion (if any) the child will be raised with

- The type of schooling and social/cultural activities the child will have

- Major decisions about the child's health

For example, the custodial parent makes the decision about whether to take the child to a doctor when the child has a cold. The joint guardian becomes involved if a decision has to be made about whether or not the child should have surgery. As well, unless otherwise indicated, the guardian will step into the shoes of the custodial parent upon that parent's death or incapacity.

Note that guardianship is not a term used in the federal Divorce Act. The Divorce Act gives the custodial parent the sole responsibility for making major decisions about the child's life, unless joint custody is ordered. Under provincial law in most provinces and territories, parents are joint guardians until one of them becomes the sole custodial parent. However, a court order or separation agreement can state that the non-custodial parent is a joint guardian.

Tip

A non-custodial parent has access (or visitation) rights to the child, but cannot make day-to-day decisions about raising the child.

It's the law

When one parent has sole custody, the Divorce Act says that the non-custodial parent "has the right to make inquiries and to be given information [only], as to the health, education and welfare of the child."

Divorce Act, Section 16(5),
R.S., 1985, C. 3 (2nd Supp.)

2.3 How is custody decided?

The decision as to which parent will have primary responsibility (custody) for the child can happen in one of three ways:

- *Separation with a verbal understanding.* After one parent moves out, both parents discuss who will keep the child and they make a decision. They may or may not put their agreement into writing. This type of agreement, even if it is in writing, can be overridden and changed by a court order because the court always has the last word regarding decisions about children. The terms can also be incorporated into the court order as a consent order.

- *Written separation agreement or consent custody order.* If the parents go to a mediator, court counsellor, or lawyer and come to an understanding, the agreement will be put into writing. That agreement may be in the form of a simple custody agreement signed by both parties, or it may be a full statement of all family matters (including support, access, and custody) in the form of a legally binding separation agreement.

    The agreement, whether it is in the form of a formal separation agreement or not, may be incorporated into a consent court order.

- *Court order after a court proceeding.* Custody may be decided by court order after a hearing or trial. Some reasons for deciding on custody by court order include the following:

  - One parent may be unhappy with the way the discussions about custody are going.

  - One parent may have been left with the child without any discussion.

  - The parent who has the child may be afraid the other parent will try and take the child away from him or her without warning, and/or one parent may be threatening to take the child to another province or territory, or another country.

Definition: Consent court order

Where both parties agree on the terms, a consent court order can be drafted setting out the arrangements. Both parties then sign it either personally or by their lawyers, and the draft order is filed in the court registry. A judge then reviews the draft order without anyone having to appear in court. If the judge finds the terms acceptable in form and content, the judge will sign it and both parties will get a copy of the order.

In these cases, the situation would be more stable and secure if there was a court order giving custody to one parent. Then, if the other parent tried to take the child, the court order could be enforced by the police if necessary.

2.4 What factors are relevant in deciding who has custody?

The courts decide on custody issues by using the principle of the "best interests of the child." Parents deciding on custody issues should also use this principle. It considers the physical, emotional, material, intellectual, and moral well-being of the child, as well as his or her immediate and long-term needs for care. Parental rights, needs, and interests are secondary to the best interests of the child.

The Divorce Act states that, in deciding on custody, the court is not to consider the past conduct of any person unless the conduct is relevant to the ability of the person to act as a parent to the child. This means that extra-marital relationships or abuse of one parent by the other do not automatically rule out a parent for gaining custody in the eyes of the court.

It's the law

The Divorce Act refers to the principle of "best interests of the child" in section 16(8):

"In making an order under this section, the court shall take into consideration only the best interests of the child of the marriage as determined by reference to the condition, means, needs and other circumstances of the child."

The courts of each province or territory will interpret the best interests of the child in light of their experience with how the concept is defined and applied in their court systems. Generally, the courts will consider the following factors:

- The ability of each parent to care for the child and act as a parent

- The love, affection, and similar ties that exist between the child and each parent, and between the child and other people who reside with the child and/or who are involved in the care and upbringing of the child

- The child's health and emotional well-being, including any special needs and how they are being met

- Any history of violence by either parent

- The length of time the child has lived in a stable home environment

- The education and training provided and available to the child

- The child's preference, especially an adolescent's

- The child's cultural ties and religious affiliations

The courts usually prefer to maintain the status quo, and will often leave the child in the home where he or she has had the most recent and longest continued residence. They will also pay a great deal of attention to the stated wishes of a teenager about which parent he or she would like to live with, because teenagers are capable of moving themselves to the home they prefer. Courts also avoid separating brothers and sisters unless there are very good reasons, such as a history of living separately or a large age difference between siblings.

Increasingly, the courts are paying attention to the father's rights movement. Traditionally, it could be assumed the mother would have sole custody of a child "of tender years," but this assumption can no longer be taken for granted. The courts have begun to show a preference for an arrangement where the child is primarily resident with the mother, but with the father having the rights of joint custody and guardianship; that is, the right to be involved in decision-making about the upbringing of the child even if he spends less than half of his time with the child. This arrangement can be difficult on all concerned, however, when there hard feelings and communication difficulties.

Disagreements over custody and parenting after separation are best resolved with the intervention of counsellors, mediators, or lawyers. This is particularly true where violence or the threat of violence has been present in the family, or where one of the people in the separation refuses, at all or in a reasonable way, to discuss arrangements for the care and well-being of the child.

3. How do we arrange access?

When one parent is given sole custody of a child, the non-custodial parent must be allowed to continue to have a relationship and spend time with the child. This is known as having access to the child. If custody is joint or shared, then the concept of access does not apply because the joint custody order or agreement will set out a schedule for when the child will be residing with each parent.

Access can also be available to a person other than a parent if it is in the child's best interest, as would be the case with a relative or step-parent who has been involved in raising the child. There are few situations in which the courts are not disposed to allow access.

The courts have found it to be in the best interests of children for access visits to be as frequent as possible. It is also best when the parents arrange the times between themselves according to their schedules. This is called a "reasonable and generous access" arrangement, and is often used in court orders where the parents are able to work out a visitation schedule themselves because they are communicating well and with little acrimony.

Access can be "specified" by the court when the spouses are not communicating well or at all. In that case, the court or person assisting the spouses to come to an agreement will set out an exact schedule of visitation times. The schedule will include a

Definition: Jurisdiction

(i) The geographic boundaries within which a court has the authority to act. For example, legislation passed by a provincial government applies only within provincial boundaries.

(ii) The source of authority that has power to pass laws. For example, a provincial government has the authority to pass laws regarding the administration of the courts in the province due to the division of laws set out in the Constitution Act. In other words, the provinces and territories have jurisdiction over the administration of the court system.

system for notifying in advance the custodial parent when a scheduled visit is going to be missed.

The order might also set out that neither party can remove the child from the jurisdiction of the court without the consent of the other parent upon giving at least 30 days' notice. A big problem with access occurs when one parent wants to move a significant distance from the other. If asked to intervene, the court will decide by looking at what is in the best interests of the child. A related issue is who should pay for the transportation costs during visitation times. This is also a factor in deciding if there are grounds for deviating from the child support guidelines (see Section **4.**).

The court can also order that access be supervised if that would be in the best interests of the child. Examples include instances in which there is a history of violent or erratic behaviour around the child, or an addiction to drugs or alcohol, or when the parent has not had any contact with the child for a number of years. Supervised access is usually ordered for a time-limited period so that the parent's ability to behave appropriately with the child can be assessed.

Under the Divorce Act, the parent with access has the right to be given information by the custodial parent about the child's health, education, and well-being.

4. How is child support determined?

4.1 When is there an obligation to pay child support?

Both parents have the obligation to provide their child with the necessities of life, including adequate food, shelter, and clothing. (This obligation continues until the child is 16.) The non-custodial parent meets this obligation by paying child support. When there is a person standing in the shoes of a parent (e.g., common-law spouse, same-sex partner, or grandparent), that person is also financially obligated to support the child.

It's the law

The courts will not allow parents to agree that child support is not payable, except in very unusual circumstances.

Child support is closely related to the custody arrangements. Where there is at least a 40-60 split in care giving (i.e., each parent has custody of the child for at least 40 percent of the time), child support in accordance with the federal or provincial guidelines is not payable to the other spouse. In these cases, the parents will have to decide what kind of child support arrangements (if any) apply. If the matter is put before a judge because the parents cannot agree on an amount, the judge will apportion the total child-care expenses between the custodial parents.

If the child's primary residence is with one parent for more than 60 percent of the time, the other parent must pay him or her child support, regardless of whether the custodial parent has a higher income than the non-custodial parent.

The obligation to pay child support continues until the child reaches the age of majority (see Section **1.2** above) in the province or territory in which he or she resides. It may also continue once the child is over the age of majority if he or she is still dependent on his or her parents.

Tip

Some provincial governments have established centres for supervision of access. Some communities have a fee-based resource that arranges supervisors. A responsible family member or friend can also fill the role.

It's the law

An adult child may be dependent on his or her parents if the child is "unable, by reason of illness, disability or other cause, to withdraw from their (parents') charge or to obtain the necessaries of life."

Section 1(2) *Divorce Act* as amended in 1997

If you (custodial parent) are in the process of applying for divorce, you can still claim child support under provincial child support legislation. If you are claiming child support under the federal Divorce Act, any federal order that is made will override the provincial order.

4.2 Post-secondary education

There is no legal rule requiring child support payments to continue while a child is pursuing post-secondary education. If asked, the court looks at whether the adult child is still under parental "charge." Of course, the payment can continue when both parents agree. If the parents cannot come to an agreement, then the parent supporting the child can apply for a court order that will order the other parent to pay.

The court has the discretion to require the non-custodial parent to pay support, and to set an amount that takes into account any income the older child may be receiving from other sources as well as both parents' ability to provide support. When the adult child is living away from home, the court will decide on support payments based on the child's degree of financial and emotional dependence on his or her parents. There is no issue if the adult child has voluntarily withdrawn from parental charge.

4.3 Remarriage/second family

The responsibility to support the child of the marriage continues even if one spouse remarries. If the custodial parent remarries, the duty of the natural parent to pay child support only stops if and when the step-parent legally adopts the child. If the paying parent remarries, the amount paid to support his or her child can only be reduced where it can be shown that the standard of living of the second family is lowered as a result of having to pay child support.

4.4 What is the amount of child support payable?

Unfortunately, many women with children live at a much lower standard after divorce than they did before divorce. The courts have ruled that, as much as possible, the child should be maintained at the same standard of living as the family had before the marriage breakdown.

In an effort to deal with the increasing poverty of women and children after divorce in Canada, the federal government amended the Divorce Act in 1997. The Divorce Act now requires child support to be calculated on the basis of the standard guidelines established by the federal government in 1997 and since amended.

Tip

Go to <http://canada.justice .gc.ca/en/ps/cca/invent/main .htm> for more information on custody and support.

> **It's the law**
>
> "The guidelines are designed to make the calculation of child support fair, predictable and consistent for the benefit of the children."
>
> *Divorce Act* as amended in 1997

All the provinces and territories have adopted the guidelines. If you are calculating child support under provincial family law or under the Divorce Act, you will use the provincial tables in every province and territory except Alberta, which uses the federal tables. When the spouse who is obligated to pay (payor) lives in a different province or territory from the custodial parent, the guidelines of the payor's province or territory are to be used to calculate the amount. If the payor lives outside Canada or his or her whereabouts are unknown, then the federal guidelines are to be used.

4.5 Can the child support amount be varied?

Because the obligation to pay child support is for the benefit of the child, the parents cannot enter into an agreement, for any reason, that child support not be paid. They can, however, come to an agreement that an amount different than the guideline amount be paid as long as it is a reasonable amount. The courts may consider whether there has been an unequal division of property benefiting the custodial parent. It will also consider all the needs and circumstances of both parents.

To have the judge order a greater or lesser amount, you must have a signed separation agreement or consent order setting out the different amount agreed upon by both parents. That amount can then be incorporated into the Divorce Order.

If you are claiming for child support, your divorce documents must include either —

- a full financial statement from you or your spouse,

- a waiver to file financial statements (in some provinces and territories),

Tip

For more information on the Federal Child Support Guidelines, visit <http://canada2 .justice.gc.ca/en/ps/sup/index. html>. See the information for your province or territory on the CD-ROM at the back of this book for the child support guidelines for your location.

Tip

If you or your spouse want child support to be in an amount different than what is set by the Child Support Guidelines Table, you must give the judge sufficient details to satisfy him or her that the amount is reasonable.

- an agreement to pay child support in a given amount (in some provinces and territories), or

- affidavit evidence from both spouses giving income information (in some provinces and territories).

The divorce court judge will also consider approving an amount different from the table figure if there are special expenses or if paying the guideline amount would cause undue hardship (see below).

4.6 What are undue hardship and special expenses?

The federal Child Support Guidelines state that undue hardship and special expenses may be taken into account when calculating child support payments. When the amount of child support is different from the guideline amount, the court must be satisfied that it is a reasonable arrangement given all the circumstances.

A court can decide to lower or raise the amount of child support from the guideline amount on the grounds of undue hardship when one spouse has a significantly lower standard of living than the other spouse. This could result from an unusually large debt arising from supporting the family or earning a living. Or there could be significant access expenses (e.g., travel costs) arising from the distance the parents live from each other. Responsibility for paying for the support of children from other marriages or spousal support obligations can also be considered undue hardship.

There are four categories of special child-related expenses that can be added to the guideline amount to increase the amount of support payable if accepted by the court or the other parent. These are:

- Child-care expenses

- Extraordinary medical and health-related expenses of the child

- Extraordinary educational expenses

- Extraordinary expenses for extracurricular activities that allow a child to pursue a special interest or talent or attend a specialized program

If you or your spouse want to alter the amount set out in the guidelines because of undue hardship, special expenses, or some other valid reason, it would be best to seek legal advice either from a lawyer or from someone knowledgeable about child support who is connected with the government child support or court system in your province or territory. The forms required to support the request are complicated, and it is best to get help completing them from someone knowledgeable in the area.

4.7 How does child support affect my taxes?

The amount of child support payable is now determined by the provincial or federal guidelines. The guidelines are based on research that established that the proportion of family income devoted to the care of children is the same across all levels of income. The guidelines take into account:

- gross income levels in increments of $100 up to $150,000, and

- the number of children you have.

The amounts payable take income taxes into account.

Previously, a spouse paying child support under a written agreement or court order could deduct the expenses from his or her income tax. The spouse receiving the child support had to include the amount as income.

This situation has now changed for all new orders and agreements made after May 1, 1997. If you are paying child support under a written separation agreement or court order made after May 1, 1997, you can no longer deduct the expenses from your income tax. If you are receiving child support, you do not need to include the amount as income on your taxes.

The new tax rules do not apply automatically to orders or agreements made before May 1, 1997. They may, however, apply to those orders or agreements if —

(a) the existing order or agreement is changed on or after May 1, 1997, either to increase or decrease the amount of child support payable;

Tip

If your written agreement or consent order was made before May 1, 1997, you may be able to convert it to the new rules.

(b) the existing order or agreement specifically provides that the new tax rules will apply to all payments made after a certain date (not earlier than May 1, 1997); or

(c) both spouses sign a form T1157, Election for Child Support Payments, that confirms they elect that the new tax rules will apply some time on or after May 1, 1997 (you can obtain this form from Canada Customs and Revenue Agency).

Once your child support payments come under the new rules, you will not be permitted to return to the old system.

4.8 Child tax benefit

The child tax benefit is automatically calculated by the federal government and is paid monthly to eligible recipients. To be eligible, the child must be under the age of 18 and living with a parent who has valid immigration status (i.e., Canadian citizen, permanent resident, or convention refugee). The parent with whom the child is living and who has primary responsibility for caring for the child is eligible to receive the benefit. If the custodial parent is different from the one who received the tax benefit in the previous year, the new custodial parent must apply to receive the benefit.

The parent applying must have filed an income tax return for the previous year. The amount of the child tax benefit will be adjusted each July based on the preceding year's family income, as reported on the family's income tax returns. The benefit is not subject to income tax.

If custody is shared or if two parents have applied to receive the benefit in the same year, the Canada Customs and Revenue Agency (CCRA) will conduct a review to determine if the child actually resides with both parents. The CCRA does not rely on a court order or separation agreement as proof of shared custody. If custody is truly shared, then the CCRA will pay one parent for six months and then rotate the payments to the other parent for the next six months in an amount reflective of each income. You can request an alternate arrangement or an appeal of the CCRA's decision at any time. Visit Canada Customs and Revenue Agency at <www.ccra-adrc.gc.ca>.

Tip

If your marital status or custody arrangements change, you must file a new application for the child tax benefit.

5
Spousal Support

When is one spouse obligated to support the other?

What factors determine spousal support?

What legal assistance is available for getting spousal support?

What are the tax consequences of spousal support?

Spousal Support

1. When is one spouse obligated to support the other?

Historically, the concept of marriage included the responsibility of a husband to support his wife. In modern times, it is the law that each spouse has the responsibility to support the other. After separation, one spouse is often worse off financially than the other spouse. This is especially true where one parent is staying at home to look after children, not working at a paying job, or working part time.

To minimize the economic hardship caused by separation and divorce, the law requires the spouse with the higher earnings to continue to support the other for a time after separation. Both provincial family law and the Divorce Act provide for spousal support. The hope is that by being supported for a time after separation, the economically disadvantaged spouse will find a way to become economically self-sufficient.

Many spouses do not even consider negotiating for spousal support because they think it is too difficult. But the courts are willing to order spousal support where there is a clear economic disparity in income between the two spouses. The courts have made it clear that the amount of spousal support can always be reconsidered if the original agreement was clearly unfair or if the parties' circumstances materially change.

Definition: Spouse
One of two people who live in a marriage-like relationship, meaning the people co-habit and have a sexual component to the relationship.

Tip
The goal of spousal support is to equalize the standards of living of both parties after separation. It is particularly relevant in long-term marriages.

> **It's the law**
> The legal principles and factors used to determine spousal support are the same under the Divorce Act as under provincial legislation.

2. What factors determine spousal support?

Not many spouses will readily agree to split their income with their spouse after separation, especially since the law can require that up to 50 percent of the working spouse's income go to the other spouse for an indefinite period of time.

The amount each spouse receives as result of the division of the family assets is an important factor in determining spousal support. For this reason, spousal support should not be considered until after the family assets have been divided, including apportioning the family debt load. The amount of child support payable should also first be determined. If the amount of child support being paid leaves the paying spouse with little disposable income, the court, especially under the Divorce Act, may not order spousal support. Child support is the priority.

The extent of the obligation to pay spousal support depends on a number of other factors:

- The length of the marriage

- The contribution of each spouse to the relationship and to the cohabitation arrangement (e.g., child care, financial support of the other's business, or financial support during the other's education)

- Whether one spouse stayed home to look after the children, resulting in that spouse's loss of job opportunities and future earning power

- The financial situation of each spouse throughout the marriage

- Any agreements, orders, or arrangements relating to the support of the spouse or the children

- Whether any economic disparities were addressed by the division of property upon separation

The conduct of the spouses leading up to the separation is not a factor in assessing entitlement and amount of spousal support. The court's only interest is in ensuring that the breakup of a marriage does not put one spouse in a situation of severe economic hardship.

3. What legal assistance is available for getting spousal support?

It is often especially difficult for women to put forward their personal need for spousal support over and above child support. The law will, however, assist people who have been in long marriages and who have given up job opportunities for the sake of their children. Their spouses may be ordered to pay support until they have been through an educational or retraining program, they find a way of earning a sufficient income, or the children have left home. If the disadvantaged spouse is ill or disabled or if the marriage was of a long duration, the obligated spouse may be required to pay support permanently. The obligation will end if the disadvantaged spouse remarries.

If you need financial assistance from your former spouse, you should get legal advice to assist in spousal support negotiations. Where both parties are being fairly reasonable in their approach to the negotiations, a mediator may be helpful as a somewhat less expensive alternative to lawyers. But if one spouse is not being reasonable and not negotiating openly and in good faith, the only way to proceed is by starting a court action.

You can apply to court for spousal support for up to one or two years after the divorce, depending on your province or territory, but with difficulty. It is much better to apply before applying for divorce. Consult a lawyer if you are ready to apply for divorce but think you are entitled to spousal support.

4. What are the tax consequences of spousal support?

If you are making periodic spousal support payments under a separation agreement or consent court order, you may deduct the payments from your income taxes. If you are receiving spousal support you must claim the amounts as income.

You need to register your order or agreement if it requires payment of spousal support only, or separate amounts for spousal and child support. To do so, send the Canada Customs and Revenue Agency (CCRA) a completed copy of Form T1158, Registration of Family Support Payments, along with a copy of the order or agreement. You can find a copy of Form T1158 at <www.ccra-adrc.gc.ca/E/pub/tg/p102eq/README.html>. You

Tip

To claim the spousal support deduction, the separation agreement or court order must be registered with the Canadian Customs and Revenue Agency.

must notify CCRA if the child or spousal support payable changes from the amount originally registered.

Note: You may only deduct spousal support payments if you meet all of the following conditions:

(a) The support payments were periodic and were not one lump sum.

(b) The payments were made under a court order, judgment, or written agreement.

(c) The payments were made by you to your spouse or to his or her agent or to a third party (such as a mortgage company) for the benefit of the spouse, on a periodic basis.

(d) You were separated from your spouse at the time the first payment was made and have remained separated throughout the year.

As you can see, it is important to define in your separation agreement or consent court order that spousal support is being paid in the form of a specific sum of money at regular intervals (e.g., biweekly or monthly). This will ensure that payments are properly deductible.

Your written separation agreement is effective only from the date it is signed by all parties. However, payments made in the current year or the year preceding the signing of the written separation agreement may still be deductible if the payments were actually made and all other conditions (above) are met.

Note, that in condition (d) above, if you are considering reconciling with your spouse, you may lose the deduction for the year. Suppose you and your spouse separated according to a written agreement in February and then you got back together for the month of November in an attempt to reconcile. In this case, you would not be able to claim in your annual income tax return support payments made as a deduction because you were not separated "throughout the remainder of the year." (Reconciliation attempted in January of the following year would be much more beneficial, at least financially.) In this example, however, as you were not able to deduct the payments made from February through to November, your spouse would not have to claim them as income.

6
Matrimonial Property

How do we divide marital property?

How is the property valued?

Who gets to keep the family home?

How are Canada Pension Plan benefits split?

Should I revise my will?

Matrimonial Property

1. How do we divide marital property?

Marriage automatically entitles each spouse to share in the marital property upon the breakdown of the marriage. In determining how to divide the marital property, the law does not consider whose name is on the property as owner. The question is whether the property was used for a family purpose and whether it was intended to be family property. For example, a settlement for personal injury would not be considered a family asset.

Matrimonial property or family assets include the following:

- Debts
- Pensions
- RRSPS
- The family home
- Vehicles
- Boats
- The family (and in some cases one spouse's) business
- Recreational property

In some provinces and territories, each spouse is entitled to half of the matrimonial property, including the debts. In other provinces and territories, the property is not divided but the debts and assets owned by each spouse are valued and then an equalization payment is calculated. In all provinces and territories, if one spouse does not agree with an equal division or the

Tip

There are important time limits to asserting your legal claim for a division of family property, so talk to a lawyer before starting to work on the application for divorce.

equalization calculation, then the other spouse must either agree to an unequal division or the spouses have to go to mediation or court.

If you go to court, the provincial statutes set out what factors the judge has to consider in coming to a decision to divide the property unequally. Some factors include:

- How much property each spouse owned before the marriage
- Length of the marriage
- Any inherited property

It is up to the person who believes an equal division would not be fair to establish grounds for an unequal split.

Matrimonial property can only be dealt with under provincial family or marital property statutes. You cannot apply under the federal Divorce Act for a division of the marital property. Provincial legislation and court rules will allow you to join an action for the division of property under the provincial family legislation with a federal divorce action so that property matters can be heard at the same time as all the other family/divorce issues. Unless your spouse has signed a separation agreement or there are consent orders in place, you will need to at least consult with a lawyer to do this. The court procedures and law covering marital property are complex.

If you don't deal with property matters before the divorce, you may find that your spouse's creditors will try after the divorce to make you responsible for his or her default on debts incurred before the divorce. The bank may try to make you responsible for mortgage payments even when you no longer live in the home. Or you may lose your right to claim your entitlement to share in your spouse's pension.

In some parts of Canada, you cannot apply to the courts to settle property matters after you have filed for divorce. In other provinces and territories, you have two years from the time of the Divorce Order to start an action for division of family property, or six years from the date of separation, whichever comes first. In still other areas you must apply within 60 days of the divorce becoming final.

2. How is the property valued?

The date used for valuation purposes and to decide what property shall be considered marital property is one of the following:

- The date of separation
- The date set as the date of separation in a written, signed separation agreement
- The date set by a judge as the date of separation
- The date of the divorce

3. Who gets to keep the family home?

The family home is included in the marital property even if one spouse bought it before the marriage. If the family lived in it during the marriage and there are children of the marriage, then the person retaining custody of the children will in most cases be entitled to remain in the family home until an agreement or court order deals with it under the provincial legislation.

In some provinces and territories, the fact that the home was bought before marriage will not affect its status as a matrimonial asset. In other provinces and territories, it will be valued and any change in value since the date of marriage will be included in the settlement. In any event, both parties have a right to the home and nothing can be done regarding the home without the consent of the other spouse. This means that the mortgage cannot be changed in any way or the house sold or rented without the signature of both spouses, even after they have separated.

4. How are Canada Pension Plan benefits split?

If one or both of the spouses made contributions to the Canada Pension Plan (CPP) throughout the marriage, the Canada Pension Plan will automatically send both of you notice of your right to split the entitlement upon divorce. The notice is sent as a result of the information being recorded in the Central Divorce Registry (see Chapter 8).

Any couple who lived together for at least 12 consecutive months, who separated within the previous 4 years, or whose

Tip
Property acquired after the separation is not subject to division unless it was bought with money that ought to have been shared.

marriage ended in divorce or legal annulment is entitled to apply for what is called credit splitting. The credits are calculated on the basis of the amount of contribution to the CPP. If you tell the CPP after divorce that you wish the credits to be split, then all the CPP credits accumulated by both spouses during the time they lived together (which includes any common-law periods before marriage) are added together and the total number of credits is divided equally between them. These credits are not actually paid but are used to determine the amount of CPP benefits to which each spouse may be entitled in future.

This benefits the spouse who did not contribute (e.g., as a result of not working outside the home) or who contributed less (e.g., as a result of earning less).

5. Should I revise my will?

One often overlooked aspect of divorce is what happens to the contents of your estate that you may have left your spouse in your will. Divorce will revoke any provisions in a will where one spouse leaves the other property or makes the spouse the executor. Those provisions of the will are not valid after divorce.

You should draft a new will after separation or divorce. If you want to bequeath property to your ex-spouse after divorce, you can do it in the same manner as for anyone who is left property in a will. You should also amend or redo your will to be consistent with the terms of a separation agreement or domestic contract.

For more information on doing your will, see *Wills Guide for Canada,* another title in the Self-Counsel Legal Series.

7
Can You Do Your Own Divorce?

Can I do my own divorce?

What happens if we haven't agreed on custody, access, and support?

What happens if we haven't split our marital property?

When should I get a lawyer?

Is mediation an alternative to consulting a lawyer?

Can I handle the divorce paperwork?

What are the steps for getting a divorce and how long does it take?

What will it cost?

Can You Do Your Own Divorce?

1. Can I do my own divorce?

Many people prepare and file their divorce papers without using a lawyer. All the forms for doing your own divorce in your province or territory, as well as step-by-step instructions, are included in the kits available for download from <www.self -counsel.com>. If you choose to do your own divorce, remember that divorce law can be complicated and you will need to pay attention to detail and complete the forms correctly.

Doing your own divorce without legal advice or the help of a lawyer is best done under these circumstances:

- The ground for divorce is that you have been living separate and apart for at least one year (see Chapter 1). In some provinces and territories, you will not be able to apply for an affidavit divorce if you use any other ground.

- There are no dependent children (see Chapter 4).

- Neither spouse needs financial support from the other (see Chapter 5).

- All property (i.e., personal goods, vehicles, money, debts, RRSPs, pensions, and real estate) has been divided and both spouses are happy with the property settlement (see Chapter 6).

- You only need to ask the court to make an order for the divorce itself.

If you have children under the age of majority and have yet to make decisions about financial matters, you will still be in a

Definition: Affidavit divorce

An affidavit divorce is an uncontested divorce in which the other spouse does not file a Statement of Defense or Answer and the parties do not attend at the court to appear before a judge. An affidavit divorce is recommended if you will be preparing and filing the divorce application without a lawyer. In some provinces and territories it is known as a desk-order or desk divorce. **Note:** In some provinces, you will need to appear in court even if the divorce is uncontested.

good position to do your own divorce if you and your spouse have —

- signed a separation agreement, or
- have a court order dealing with child custody, access, and support and/or division of property, or
- have come to an agreement about any or all of these matters.

If you are financially self-sufficient, have no children dependant on you, or your spouse has been paying child support and is in agreement with the custody and support arrangements you are asking to be put in the Divorce Order, you can proceed with an affidavit divorce. You will have to file enough information with the court (ideally in the form of a separation agreement or consent court order) to satisfy the judge that the arrangements are reasonable and appropriate. In some jurisdictions in this situation, you may still have to appear in front of a judge to get your Divorce Order.

2. What happens if we haven't agreed on custody, access, and support?

The Divorce Act allows you to include applications for orders concerning matters such as custody, access, and support in your divorce application. While you do not have to ask the court to deal with these other matters, if they are included in the Divorce Order they can be enforced in every province and territory of Canada.

You should seek legal advice if any or all of these issues are still unsettled at the time you decide to apply for divorce. Without legal advice, you may not realize the extent of what you are entitled to upon separation, especially if you or you and your children will be financially disadvantaged by the separation and divorce. (See Chapter 4: Children and Chapter 5: Spousal Support.)

You will definitely need legal advice if there are family assets of any value such as pensions or real estate that must be divided. You should also consider the tax consequences arising from separation and divorce.

3. What happens if we haven't split our marital property?

Matrimonial property or family assets cannot be dealt with under the Divorce Act. They must be dealt with under provincial family or marital property statutes. Some provincial legislation and court rules will allow you to join an action under the provincial family legislation with a divorce action so that property matters can be heard at the same time as all the other family and divorce issues. (See Chapter 2 for more on provincial and federal legislation.)

In some provinces, you can deal with property issues after your divorce has been finalized, though you must be careful of limitation periods.

Unless your spouse has signed a separation agreement or there are consent orders in place, if you have unsettled property matters you will likely not be able to do your own divorce without the help of a lawyer.

See Chapter 6 for more information on marital property.

4. When should I get a lawyer?

In some situations, it may be more appropriate for you to consult a lawyer and use his or her knowledge and skills, rather than to attempt to do your own divorce. You may need the services of a lawyer in any of the following situations:

Service problems :

- Your spouse resides outside Canada.

- You don't know the address of your spouse, despite having used a tracing service.

- Your spouse is actively avoiding being served.

Family situations:

- You and your spouse have not come to any agreement on child custody and access, and there have been no court orders regarding children.

Definition: Corollary relief
Applications to the court for orders concerning custody, access, and support are called requests for corollary relief or ancillary relief.

Tip
For more information on the tax aspects of divorce, see the tax sections of the following chapters:
- Chapter 4: Children
- Chapter 5: Spousal Support
- Chapter 6: Matrimonial Property

- You and your spouse are separated and you do not want your spouse to know where you reside.

Financial problems:

- Your spouse has refused to disclose income and/or the details of his or her finances.

- Your spouse won't agree to pay support either for your child(ren) or yourself (if you are in financial need) or for both of you.

- You and your spouse have not been able to come to an agreement about the division of property or debts.

Consent problems:

- Your spouse has told you that he or she will be contesting or opposing your application for divorce.

In each of these situations, a lawyer can help you deal with the problem. Many lawyers can be hired to work on just one or two aspects of the case. They will quote either a flat fee or give you an estimate of how many hours of work your case is likely to require. The only situation in which a lawyer may be required to take over the whole case is when your spouse is going to oppose the divorce and all the related issues up to and including a court trial.

When you hire a lawyer, you have to pay him or her an initial advance. This advance payment is called a retainer.

At the time you pay the retainer, most lawyers will have you sign a retainer agreement. The retainer agreement is a contract between you and the lawyer setting out the following:

- The hourly rate

- The method of payment (e.g., monthly or quarterly or when billed after each service is completed)

- The out-of-pocket expenses you are expected to pay for (e.g., court filing fees, photocopying, process serving)

- What the lawyer will be doing for you

- When and how services will be terminated

Once you have signed the retainer agreement, you are said to have retained the lawyer and his or her services. The retainer will be kept in the lawyer's trust account and transferred to his or her general account after enough work has been done to bill you for the amount of the retainer. If there is still ongoing work, the lawyer will bill you in accordance with the terms in the retainer agreement.

Some retainers are calculated on a flat rate — for example, $500 to draft the divorce application, file it, and arrange for service of the respondent.

5. Is mediation an alternative to consulting a lawyer?

Mediation is a process for settling disagreements. When two people cannot come to an agreement, they may hire a mediator to help them discuss their problems. Mediators are trained professionals. Some are also lawyers (but never for the people with whom they are acting as mediator), some are psychologists, and some are former managers.

The courts of some provinces and territories have government-funded agencies (such as the Family Justice Centres in B.C., the Family Information Centres in Ontario, and the Counselling and Mediation Services in Newfoundland and Labrador). These agencies often have trained counsellors who attempt to mediate between spouses — although they may not have the training of people who work solely as professional mediators.

The role of a mediator is to make it easier for two or more people to talk to one another and be heard. They are skilled at understanding what people are really trying to say. They are also trained to diffuse tensions and help people actually listen to each other. Mediators do not make decisions for people or tell them what to think or do. Their job is to help people come to their own decisions and make their own agreements. They cannot legally divorce people or make legally binding separation agreements for them.

5.1 When is mediation appropriate?

Mediation is a good option for separating spouses either before the separation or after they have been apart for a while. The

Tip

If a mediator is also a lawyer, he or she cannot represent either of the parties in the mediation.

process can help them make decisions about issues such as how to provide for their children and how to divide their property. The process can be used for a number of issues or just one.

Mediation will only work if both spouses are in agreement that mediation is appropriate for them. Private mediators have to be paid, so the questions of who will pay the mediator (as much as $300 a session) and which mediator to use have to be decided first. If the spouses can't get past these first steps, then mediation is clearly not appropriate. (Some Family Courts do provide free mediation services.)

Another consideration is whether there is a power imbalance in the relationship. If one spouse easily gets angry and/or abusive and then doesn't listen, mediation is not going to be possible. Or if one spouse is still at the stage of being very emotional and easily moved to tears, mediation is not going to be effective. Both people have to be ready to talk and listen calmly to what the other person has to say.

5.2 Can a mediator draft a separation agreement?

A mediator can replace some but not all of what a lawyer does. A mediator will want the spouses to identify what the outstanding issues are between them and how each spouse wants to resolve the issues. If the mediator is successful in assisting the parties to compromise and come to an agreement, then a written separation agreement would be the best outcome. Mediators sometimes help spouses write down their agreement, but not in a legally binding document.

An agreement written with the help of a mediator will not be legally binding unless each spouse has received independent legal advice to ensure that each spouse fully understands his or her legal rights and responsibilities outside the mediation process. A binding separation agreement also has to be properly signed in front of witnesses.

Mediators cannot advise you on the various areas of law. Mediators will assume that you are aware of the impact of the law on your situation. It is best if each spouse goes to his or her own lawyer to discuss his or her rights, responsibilities, and obligations *before* going to mediation.

Tip
See Chapter 3 for more information on separation agreements.

6. Can I handle the divorce paperwork?

Doing your own divorce is appropriate where there are no complications (see sections above) and you are mentally and emotionally able to focus on detailed written work. You'll need to follow all the instructions and accurately complete the court forms exactly in the format provided. You have to provide a Marriage Certificate (see Chapter 8) in the proper form. If child or spousal support is being requested, then you and your spouse should also be prepared to file financial statements and income tax returns.

The first form you complete will ask for the following detailed information:

- Identification information for both spouses and children under the age of majority (or, if older, dependent on you for their support)

- Information about the date and place of marriage

- Details of the marriage breakdown and grounds for divorce, including the date of separation

- Information about who the children reside with, who supports them, the amount of child support being paid, and the amount of arrears if any

- Terms of custody, access, and support being asked for

- An explanation of what has happened to the family property (assets and debts)

- Information about any family court proceedings, consent orders, or separation agreement

You also have to set out what you are asking the court to order (e.g., divorce, custody, support, and access), and the exact language of the terms you want included in the order.

The forms ask for information to be given in a very particular and precise way. You then take the completed forms to the court registry for checking and filing. Even lawyers have their forms rejected from time to time for not being precise enough or for being inaccurate. The registry staff are not there to provide legal advice and are very cautious when asked questions by people

Tip

The divorce application has a different name in different provinces and territories. It may be called the Statement of Claim or the Petition for Divorce.

Tip

The more professional your completed forms look and the more precise your questions are to the staff, the more likely they are to be helpful. You should try using a computer or typewriter to complete your forms. If you do not have access to any of these, then neatly print (do not write).

doing their own divorces. The staff makes every effort to be helpful, but there are limits on how many and what type of questions they will answer.

You also have to pay the court filing fees and fill in a Registration of Divorce Proceedings (some courts do it for you) for the Central Divorce Registry in Ottawa. If you are not proceeding jointly with your spouse, then you have to arrange to have your spouse personally served by a professional process server or by a friend. After waiting the required number of days to see if your spouse will file a response, you have to prepare and file the documents necessary for a judge to sign a Divorce Order. (See Chapter 8 for more information about service.)

7. What are the steps for getting a divorce and how long does it take?

There is no simple answer to how long it takes to get an affidavit divorce. Most lawyers will suggest a time of three to six months from beginning to end of the divorce proceedings.

Once you have filed the application for a Divorce Order, the time it takes to get the Divorce Order varies depending on —

- how busy the court is,

- whether a personal appearance in front of a judge is necessary, and

- whether or not your application gets rejected and has to be resubmitted.

This process can take between one and three months.

Once the judge has signed the Divorce Order, you cannot get remarried until —

- 31 days have passed (your ex-spouse has 31 days to file an appeal to the Court of Appeal), and

- you have applied for and received the Certificate of Divorce. (This is the document needed to prove that you are divorced.)

See the flowchart on page 70.

Tip

If you are using separation for one year as grounds for a divorce, you can start the proceedings but cannot be granted the divorce before the one-year period is up.

8. What will it cost?

Even if you don't use a lawyer, getting a divorce costs money. If there are no problems in your case, the expenses will probably add up to about $350. If you can't afford the filing fee, most courts allow you to file without a fee. Ask the registry staff if this is possible. It may be possible if you are on social assistance or you earn wages that are close to the social assistance rates. This is called indigent status.

You can also ask your spouse to pay some or all of the expenses. The court rules allow you to include a request for "costs" in your application for divorce. If the court ordered your spouse to pay costs, however, you would be responsible for collecting the money from him or her.

The figures below are approximations only. The courts of each province and territory have their own fee schedules, and you should check with registry staff to see what the actual fees are. In some provinces and territories, there are no fees after you have paid the court filing fee. In other provinces, you pay the filing fee and a fee for the Divorce Order only. In most provinces and territories, you must pay an additional fee if you wish to obtain a Certificate of Divorce. The fees for each province and territory can be found in the step-by-step procedures in the kits available for download from <www.self-counsel.com>.

Certificate of Marriage	$20
Application for Search of Central Divorce Registry	$0 – $10
Court filing fee:	
Application	$70 – $218
Divorce Order	$0 – $280
Substitutional service	$100
Certificate of Divorce	$30
Tracing service	$150 – $400
Professional process service	$30 – $75
Affidavit of Service	$25 – $50
Swearing Affidavits	$0 – $50

Tip

Even lawyers have their applications rejected at times. These are some reasons why registry staff may reject your documents:

- They are messy (particularly if handwritten)

- You have not answered all the questions

- You have given answers that are long and hard to understand (i.e., you haven't followed the standard form of answer)

- All the paperwork is not there (e.g., you refer to a separation agreement but don't attach it)

- The pages are not in the standard format because you retyped the forms and rearranged paragraphs or made the margins too small or too big

FLOWCHART FOR UNDEFENDED DIVORCE PROCEDURE

Obtain Marriage Certificate and prepare court application
(Statement of Claim or Petition) for a divorce.

Decide if filing as sole or joint.

Take divorce application to court registry for filing.
(The registry opens a file and returns the original or true copies to you.)

Registry notice filed and cleared by the Central Divorce Registry in Ottawa.
Up to 8 weeks.

Sole applicants only: Serve the divorce papers on your spouse.

Check with the registry to determine if the Clearance Certificate from the
Central Divorce Registry in Ottawa is ready.

Sole applicants only:
Wait the required period to see if your spouse files a response.
If your spouse files a response contesting the Petition, you should consult a lawyer.
7 to 60 days (depending on your province or territory and where your spouse lives).

If your spouse does not file a response or if you are proceeding jointly,
prepare documents for the application for the Divorce Order or Judgment.
Have your Affidavits sworn by a notary or commissioner of oaths.

Take the documents to the court registry.
The registry checks the documents and rejects or accepts them.

The registry puts your file before a judge, who will accept or reject them.
(You may have to appear in court in some provinces.)

Retrieve the Divorce Order or Judgment from the registry or wait for it to be
mailed to you by the court. If they were rejected, review the comments, correct them,
and return the documents to the registry.

If the documents were accepted and the Divorce Order was signed,
wait 31 days before applying for the divorce certificate.
(In some provinces and territories the court mails the certificate to you without an application.)
(1 to 2 weeks)

8
Getting Started: The Basics

Which court registry do I use?

What if we weren't married in Canada?

How do I get my Marriage Certificate?

Who starts the divorce?

Should I file as a joint or sole applicant?

What if my spouse files a response to the application?

How do I register the divorce?

How do I serve the papers on my spouse?

Can I change my name?

How do I apply for the Divorce Order?

How do I get a Certificate of Divorce?

Getting Started: The Basics

Each province and territory has different procedures for getting a divorce. However, regardless of where you live and in which province or territory you will start your divorce, there are some basic elements that are common to all the provinces and territories. This chapter outlines some of these elements. For more information on the procedures in your specific province or territory, see the step-by-step procedures outlined in the kits available for download from <www.self-counsel.com>.

1. Which court registry do I use?

You should file the application for divorce in the province or territory in which you are ordinarily resident. This is the province or territory where you have been living for at least one year before filing for divorce. You can leave the province or territory for a period or periods of time during the year (e.g., to go on vacation or on a training course), but you must have maintained your home and connection to the province or territory for the year.

If you have not been ordinarily resident in the province in which your spouse has been living, you can still start your divorce in that province. Only one of you has to have been ordinarily resident in a particular province for the one-year period.

Each province and territory has rules about which court registry you should use to file your application. Generally, you should file in the court registry that is located nearest to where you live. If you live in New Brunswick, you can only file in Fredericton. If you live in Prince Edward Island, you can only file in Charlottetown.

Tip

See Chapter 7 for a step-by-step outline of getting a divorce.

Definition: Court registry

The registry is the office (most often) located on the main floor of the court house. It includes the counter where the registry staff serves the public who come to file or pick up court documents. In the central court house in the large judicial districts, there may be a separate counter for a civil registry, a divorce registry, a probate registry, a criminal registry, and an appeals registry. The registry is also the repository of all the court records (the files opened for each case).

You have to give your residential address on the divorce application forms. If you have reason to fear your spouse and he or she does not have the address of your residence, then you may use the address of a lawyer, legal aid office, or transition house. You may have to discuss this option with the court registry staff and with the office whose address you wish to use.

If you are filing as a sole applicant, the location of your spouse's place of residence does not matter. The only consideration arising from your spouse's place of residence is how difficult it will be for you to serve him or her (see Section **8.** below).

If your spouse lives in another country with the child of the marriage, you must consult a lawyer to determine which country is the appropriate place to start the divorce action.

2. What if we weren't married in Canada?

If you were married outside Canada you can be divorced in Canada even if you are not a permanent resident or citizen of Canada. The rule is that one spouse must have lived (been ordinarily resident as defined in Section **1.** above) in a province or territory of Canada for the 12 months before filing the application for divorce.

You will have to file an original Marriage Certificate from the government of the country where you were married, along with a translation in a form acceptable to the local court registry. Check with your court for what they require to prove foreign marriages. Some provinces and territories have a different requirement for the United States and British Commonwealth countries than for other foreign countries.

3. How do I get my Marriage Certificate?

You must file an original certificate of your marriage or a certified copy of the registration of your marriage at the court registry when you start the divorce. An original certificate must be issued by the government and must be the original sent to you from the government office where you obtained it. A church document or record of solemnization is not considered proof of the marriage.

To get a Marriage Certificate for a marriage in Canada, phone or write the government department — usually called Vital Statistics or Office of the Registrar General — in the province or territory where you were married. (See the Appendix for a list of the Vital Statistics offices and Web sites in your province or territory.) You will have to pay the applicable fee.

The government office will issue one in the appropriate form if you indicate that it is needed for divorce purposes.

If the certificate is not in English or French, the original Marriage Certificate or a certified true copy and a translation must be filed with the application for divorce. The translator must swear in an affidavit that he or she translated the document. Ensure that you use a qualified court translator.

Your application for divorce will not be accepted unless the Marriage Certificate is presented. The court will check that the names and other information on the divorce application match the information on the Marriage Certificate. If there is a discrepancy, you must give an explanation.

If you can't produce your Marriage Certificate or a certified copy of the registration, the registrar can use discretion to accept an explanation and file your documents if he or she is satisfied with the reasons you have set out in the court divorce documents.

An acceptable reason might be the loss or destruction of the original records of marriage by fire or other disaster in the country where you were married. In such a case, you will have to provide an affidavit with evidence of the place and time of marriage at the time of the application for the Divorce Order. A church document would be a good attachment to such an affidavit.

4. Who starts the divorce?

If the ground for divorce is that you have lived separate and apart for one year, then either spouse may start the divorce process. Of course, if the ground is adultery or cruelty, then the offended party is the one who has to apply for divorce.

When the divorce is started, the spouse filing the papers may be called the petitioner or plaintiff (depending on the procedure

Definition: Registrar

The person hired by the court to manage the registry, which houses the court files and the desk where the public attends to file applications.

Definition: Joint application

A joint application is a request to the court for a divorce by consent. Both spouses agree on all the terms of the divorce.

Definition: Minutes of settlement

The written record of an out-of-court settlement of the outstanding issues before the court. It is drawn up by the lawyers in the appropriate form for filing in the court to conclude the case.

in your province or territory). The other spouse is called the respondent or defendant (depending on the procedure in your province or territory). If your province or territory allows joint applications, then both husband and wife may be the petitioners or co-petitioners.

5. Should I file as a joint or sole applicant?

In all provinces and territories except Alberta and Newfoundland and Labrador, both spouses can start the divorce together if the ground is separation for one year. This is called a joint application.

In the provinces and territories that have established a court procedure for filing for joint divorce, the application can only be for divorce or, if there are other issues, there must be consent orders or a separation agreement already in place. One advantage of a joint application is that there does not have to be service of the documents on the other spouse, since both parties are signing the documents to start the application. Both parties also have to sign the affidavits in support of the application for the order. These affidavits have to be dated at the time of applying for judgment and not at the time of signing the writ or petition.

See Chapter 1 for more information on joint applications.

6. What if my spouse files a response to the application?

Once you have filed the divorce papers on your spouse, he or she may do one of the following:

- Choose not to file a response to the divorce. You will have to wait the time specified by your province's or territory's rules to see if your spouse will file a response before you can proceed with your application for a Divorce Order. (See the step-by-step procedures for your province or territory in the kits available for download from <www.self-counsel.com> for the applicable waiting period.)

- File a response or defence at the court. The response will be filed using a form called an Answer or a Statement of

Defence. The response must be served on you (the applicant) within the time limits set by the court in your province or territory.

Note that by filing a response, your spouse cannot stop the divorce itself, but he or she can contest aspects of the divorce application. The application then changes from an affidavit divorce to a contested proceeding. When this happens, the case goes on the contested list at the court house and a trial date is set. To continue with the divorce, the parties must either —

- come to an agreement about the contested issues, withdraw the response, and file a consent or minutes of settlement with the court, or

- go to trial, where a judge will make a decision on the issues.

If your spouse has filed a response, it would be best to consult a lawyer because the court procedures do get complicated.

7. How do I register the divorce?

All applications for divorce are recorded at the Central Divorce Registry in Ottawa. The registry is managed by the Department of Justice. This registry ensures that spouses living in different parts of Canada do not both proceed with a divorce at the same time or after one has already been started. The Divorce Act sets out rules for deciding which divorce will proceed if two are filed at the same time.

When you file your application, you will complete a form (supplied by the court registry) for registering your divorce. This form is used to conduct a search of the Central Divorce Registry. There is a $10 fee for registration (except in Ontario, where the fee is $26, as Ontario has its own system). In most provinces, this fee is in the court filing fee. An application for a Divorce Order cannot be processed until a clearance certificate that shows the results of the search of the registry has gone to your court registry. This search can take up to eight weeks.

Definition: Serve, service
Procedure for delivering the court documents into the hands of the other party. Personal service is required for the Writ of Summons and Statement of Claim or the Petition for Divorce. Personal service must be by an adult who is not a party to the divorce. He or she must confirm the service by making a sworn statement (an affidavit) that the proper person received the documents. In some provinces and territories, the person served is asked to sign an Acknowledgment of Service.

Tip

You may be able to apply for an extension of the time for service; check with your local court registry.

8. How do I serve the papers on my spouse?

When you file an application for divorce, your case will remain open at the registry until your divorce is final. However, if you are filing as a sole applicant, you must serve your spouse the divorce papers within a certain time period, or the papers will expire. Each province and territory has a different period before the papers expire. See the step-by-step procedures for your province or territory in the kits available for download from <www.self-counsel.com> for more information.

Time within which divorce papers must be served:

Alberta	12 months
B.C.	12 months
Manitoba	6 months
New Brunswick	6 months
Newfoundland and Labrador	90 days
Northwest Territories	12 months
Nova Scotia	60 days
Ontario	230 days
Prince Edward Island	6 months
Saskatchewan	6 months
Yukon	No limit

If you are the sole petitioner, you may not serve your spouse the court documents yourself. You can have a friend or relative serve the documents, as long as he or she is not a minor. He or she must swear an affidavit stating how he or she identified the person being served and the details of the service. The exact form and contents vary from province to province. (Some provinces and territories require the server to sign an Acknowledgment of Service.)

You can also use a professional process server. This is the best method of service if your spouse lives in another city. If you are using a professional process server, he or she may need a photograph of the person to be served for identification purposes. The professional server will also give you back a signed Affidavit of Service in the appropriate form for filing with the court.

In most provinces and territories, "service" means handing the filed court documents into the hands of the person named as the respondent or defendant, although some provinces allow service by mail as long as the person is prepared to return an Acknowledgment of Receipt card. You will need to have an address or phone number for the spouse who needs to be served. The information can be for his or her residence or place of business or employment. See the section below if you do not have an address for your spouse.

8.1 Efforts to locate

If you do not know where your spouse is, the most effective way to find him or her is often the most obvious: telephone or write and ask his or her friends or relatives. Depending on the length of time since the separation, you could also check with his or her work colleagues or place of employment.

If the place where you suspect your spouse is living is a relatively small city or town, you could place an advertisement in a local newspaper asking for information about your spouse from anyone who knows him or her. You could also consider hiring a skip tracer, also known as a tracing service. A skip tracer is similar to a private detective. They often work for collection agencies. He or she searches credit bureaus and government agencies for information. The cost for a skip tracer is relatively low, depending on how far and how deeply you want him or her to search. The fee is usually between $125 and $400.

8.2 Application for substitutional service

If you do not have an address for your spouse and have made every effort to locate him or her, then you may have to make an application to the court for an order allowing for substitutional service. Substitutional service means that you want to substitute another method of service in place of the requirement for personal service.

Tip

Substitutional service is common where you know where your spouse lives but not where he or she works, and you can never find him or her at home in order to serve the papers.

Definition: Substitutional service

Service of court documents on a party by a method other than by personally handing over the documents. This type of service may be by a notice in a newspaper or on a bulletin board at the court house advising the person that a court proceeding has been started. Alternatively, the court may order that the person be served by handing the documents to an adult who lives at the same address. Or the court may allow the documents to be sent by registered mail to the last known address.

Where you know your spouse's address and still can't serve him or her, your application for substitutional service might ask that the papers simply be left on the door or with any person residing with him or her at that address. It might also ask the court for permission to advertise in the paper where you think he or she last worked or resided, or leave the divorce papers with a close relative or associate of the missing spouse, or post the application papers in the local court house.

In all applications for substitutional service, you will have to make a statement in writing (an affidavit) sworn before a lawyer or notary public or commissioner for taking oaths. In that statement you will set out the efforts you made to locate your spouse.

There is a fee for making the application (usually by filing a form called a Notice of Motion) and in most provinces and territories you will have to appear in front of a judge in chambers. It is best to hire a lawyer to handle this part of your case as you cannot proceed with your application for divorce until you serve your spouse.

9. Can I change my name?

After divorce, a married woman can revert to the surname she used before marriage. Most provinces do not require a court order. Each province and territory has a different procedure for doing this, so check the step-by-step instructions in the kits available for download from <www.self-counsel.com>. The rules for change of name are available at the same Web sites or from the same addresses as those listed for marriage certificates in the Appendix.

The custodial parent can also change the surname of the child at the time of divorce as long as the other parent gives his or her consent in writing. If consent cannot be obtained, then, in most provinces and territories, the custodial parent has to apply to the court for permission to change the child's surname. The request to the court can be included in the application for divorce. The applicant has to give affidavit evidence as to why consent cannot be obtained and why it is in the best interests of the child to have the surname changed. If the child is over the age of 12, that child must also give written consent.

Tip
The forms used for the application for the Divorce Order must be signed and dated at the time you file them. They will be rejected if they have been signed prior to the divorce application being filed.

10. How do I apply for the Divorce Order?

After your spouse has been served, there is a period of time set by the court for him or her to file a response or answer (see Section **8.** above). At the end of that time period you can file the documents asking the court to sign the Divorce Order. However, most courts do not allow you to file those documents until the clearance certificate from the Central Divorce Registry in Ottawa has come through (see Section **7.** above).

The documents to be filed in support of the application for divorce vary from province to province and from territory to territory, but at a minimum include a sworn statement (affidavit) by the applicant and proof of service. In this affidavit, the applicant swears that the facts set out in the Statement of Claim or Petition for Divorce are true, and confirms the details regarding custody, access, support, and division of property (if those matters or any of them are mentioned in the Statement of Claim or Petition). The applicant must also provide the court with the order being sought in the proper form so that the judge can sign it.

Once the documents have been filed and accepted by the registry staff, the length of time it takes the judge to sign will vary from court to court. You may be asked to appear if the court rules require it or if the judge has questions after reading the documents. Or you can ask to appear if you want to avoid the delay caused by affidavit divorce processing times.

11. How do I get a Certificate of Divorce?

Once the judge signs the order, you have to wait 31 days before you can remarry. At the end of the 31 days you can apply for a Certificate of Divorce, which proves that the divorce is final. The waiting period is to ensure that no appeal has been filed and that neither spouse has changed his or her mind. There are special circumstances in which you can apply as part of your application for the Divorce Order to have the divorce take effect immediately without the 31-day delay. Examples of circumstances are when the wife in a religious family is pregnant and about to give birth, or when one of the parties has a date set for leaving the country permanently.

Tip
The Divorce Order is called the Divorce Judgment in some provinces and territories.

Remarriage, or having a date set for the wedding, will not be considered a special circumstance. Each judge exercises his or her own discretion in deciding if special circumstances exist to waive the 31-day period. Note that the 31-day waiting period is waived only in extreme situations.

Appendix
Addresses to Write to for Marriage and Birth Certificates

You will need a certificate as proof of a valid marriage in many of the proceedings described in this book. Write to the appropriate address below.

Alberta
Government Services, Alberta Registries
Vital Statistics
Box 2023
Edmonton, Alberta T5J 4W7
Telephone: (780) 427-7013 (recording)
www3.gov.ab.ca/gs/services/vpe/

British Columbia
Division of Vital Statistics Ministry of Health
818 Fort Street
Victoria, BC V8W 1H8
Telephone: 1-800-663-8328
Fax: (250) 952-1829
www.hlth.gov.bc.ca/vs

Manitoba
Division of Vital Statistics
Community Services
254 Portage Avenue
Winnipeg, MB R3C 0B6
Telephone: (204) 945-8177
(204) 945-3701 (recording)
www.gov.mb.ca/cca/vital/index.html

New Brunswick
Registrar General
Division of Vital Statistics
Department of Gov't Services and Lands
Centennial Building
Box 6000
Fredericton, NB E3B 5H1
Telephone: (506) 453-2385
www.gnb.ca/0379/en/index.htm

Newfoundland and Labrador
Vital Statistics
Government Service Centre
Department of Government Services & Lands
5 Mews Place, P.O. Box 8700
St. John's, NF A1B 4J6
Telephone: (709) 729-3308
Fax: (709) 729-0946
www.gov.nf.ca/gsl/gs/vs/

Northwest Territories
Registrar General
Vital Statistics
Department of Health and Social Services
Government of NWT
Bag 9
Inuvik, NT X0E 0T0
Telephone: (867) 777-7420
Fax: (867) 777-3197

Nova Scotia
Deputy Registrar General
1723 Hollis Street
Box 157
Halifax, NS B3J 2M9
Telephone: (902) 424-4381
(902) 424-4380 (recording)
www.gov.ns.ca/bacs/vstat

Nunavut
Registrar General of Vital Statistics
Nunavut Health and Social Services
Bag #3
Rankin Inlet, NT X0C 0G0
Telephone: (867) 645-5002
Toll-free (800) 661-0833
Fax: (867) 645-2997
www.gov.nu.ca

Ontario
Office of the Registrar General
Box 4600
189 Red River Road
Thunder Bay, ON P7B 6L8
Telephone: (416) 325-8305
In Ontario call: 1-800-461-2156
www.ccr.gov.on.ca/mcbs/english/births&marriages.htm

Prince Edward Island
Division of Vital Statistics
Department of Health & Community Services
35 Douses Road, Box 3000
Montague, PE C0A 1R0
Telephone: (902) 838-0880 or (902) 838-0881
Fax: (902) 838-0883
www.gov.pe.ca/vitalstatistics

Quebec
Direction de l'etat civil
Ministere des Relations avec les citoyens et de l'Immigration
205, rue Montmagny
Quebec, QC G1N 2Z9
Telephone: (418) 643-3900
http://www.etatcivil.gouv.qc.ca/

Saskatchewan
Division of Vital Statistics
Department of Health
1942 Hamilton Street
Regina, SK S4P 3V7
Telephone: (306) 787-3092
www.health.gov.sk.ca/ps_vital_statistics.html

Yukon Territories
Registrar of Vital Statistics
Box 2703
Whitehorse, YT Y1A 2C6
Telephone: (403) 667-5207
www.hss.gov.yk.ca

Children born abroad to armed forces personnel:

Contact the Canadian Ambassador of the country where the birth occurred. If one is not available, contact the Canadian Consulate in that country.

Children born abroad to Canadian parents:

Citizenship Registration
196 George Street
Box 7000
Sydney, NS B1P 6V6

Persons born in countries that have no Consulate in Canada

Case Management Section (JPDO)
Consular Affairs Bureau
Department of Foreign Affairs and International Trade
125 Sussex Drive
Ottawa, ON K1A 0G2
Telephone: (613) 992-1152
Fax: (613) 996-5358

Glossary

Affidavit

An affidavit is a numbered set of statements of fact, written in your own words, that you know to be true. The affidavit must be signed before a commissioner for oaths, a notary public, or a lawyer. That person will ask you to swear an oath or affirm that the information given in the affidavit is true to the best of your knowledge. It is a crime to swear an affidavit that contains false statements. The affidavit can be used in any court proceeding as evidence that the facts set out in it are believed or known to be true by the person who has sworn the affidavit.

Affidavit divorce

An affidavit divorce is an undefended divorce in which the parties do not attend at the court to appear before a judge. An affidavit divorce is recommended if you will be preparing and filing the divorce application without a lawyer. In some provinces and territories it is known as a desk-order or desk divorce.

Child of the marriage

Any child under the age of majority or dependent upon either spouse to whom the married couple/spouses act as parents. This includes children who are not biologically related to the spouses, such as step-children and children who are adopted.

Civil procedure

Each provincial government has regulations that set out the court procedure to be followed. These regulations are called the Rules of Court and have to be followed for all legal proceedings in that province or territory.

The Rules of Court set out all aspects of the procedures that must be followed when using the civil and family courts — from the type and form of all court documents to notice requirements, fees, and type of proceedings that may be brought in the different courts.

Consent court order

Where both parties agree on the terms, a consent court order can be drafted setting out the arrangements. Both parties then sign it either personally or by their lawyers and the draft order is filed in the court registry. A judge then reviews the draft order without anyone having to appear in court. If the judge finds the terms acceptable in form and content, the judge will sign it and both parties will get a copy of the order.

Contest

To oppose, dispute, or challenge through legal procedures. When a divorce is contested, one spouse challenges some terms of the application for divorce by filing a Response with the court (known as an Answer in some provinces and territories and a Statement of Defence in others). The divorce must then go on the trial list for a judge to decide on the issues being disputed.

Corollary relief

Applications to the court for orders concerning custody, access, and support are called requests for corollary relief or ancillary relief.

Court

Refers to the court house, the building housing the court rooms, the judge's chambers (offices), and the court registry. The word is also an impersonal and powerful way of referring to the judge, as in "this court orders..." or "the court decided... ."

Court registry

The registry is the office (most often) located on the main floor of the court house. It includes the counter where the registry staff serves the people who come to file or pick up court documents. In the central court house in the large judicial districts, there may be a separate counter for a civil registry, a divorce registry, a probate registry, a criminal registry, and an appeals registry. The registry is also the repository of all the court records (the files opened for each case).

Custodial parent

The parent who has custody of the child. Custody means the parent has responsibility for the care and control of the child; that is, the child lives with that parent.

If there is a court order for custody, the court may have ordered that both parents have custody, with primary residence of the child being with one parent. If there is no court order or agreement, both parents have the right to custody, but the parent with whom the child lives is in fact the custodial parent.

Divorce

A decision of a judge (in the form of an order or judgment) ending a marriage. The order is made under the authority given the court by the federal Divorce Act.

Executed

To execute a contract means to complete a contract in proper form. For a separation agreement to be legal, it must be dated, signed, witnessed, and, in some provinces and territories, a certificate of independent legal advice must be attached.

Hearing

A court proceeding in which one or both parties appear in front of the judge or other court official (e.g., registrar or master) assigned to their case. The proceeding may be a trial or it may be a procedural application. The judge, registrar, or master hears the evidence, which is presented either in the form of affidavits or sworn oral testimony. The parties also make oral argument to convince the judge to make a decision that will favour one side or the other.

Joint application

A joint application is a request to the court for a divorce by consent. Both spouses agree on all the terms of the divorce. Not available in Newfoundland or Alberta.

Jurisdiction

(i) The geographic boundaries within which a court has the authority to act. For example, legislation passed by a provincial government only applies within provincial boundaries.

(ii) The source of authority that has power to pass laws. For example, a provincial government has the authority to pass laws regarding the administration of the courts in the province due to the division of laws set out in the Constitution Act. In other words, the provinces and territories have jurisdiction over the administration of the court system.

Matter

Any case or proceeding entered on the records of a court, and to be proved by the production of such record, such as trials, motions, applications, affidavit divorces, pre-trials, teleconferences, case management, support enforcement hearings, etc.

Minutes of settlement

The written record of an out-of-court settlement of the outstanding issues before the court. It is drawn up by the lawyers in the appropriate form for filing in the court to conclude the case.

Parental charge

When a child is under parental charge, it means that the adult child is still accepting direction from the custodial parent.

Party, parties

The two or more people involved in the court action. The person starting the action is called the plaintiff or petitioner. The person being served is called the defendant or respondent.

Reconciliation

When the married couple who has separated move back together in an effort to settle their differences and to make the marriage work. Under the Divorce Act, the period of living together for this purpose has to be less than 90 days during the one-year period immediately preceding the order for divorce.

Registrar

The person hired by the court to manage the registry, which houses the court files and the desk where the public attends to file applications.

Serve, service

Procedure for delivering the court documents into the hands of the other party. Personal service is required for the Writ of Summons and Statement of Claim or the Petition for Divorce. Personal service must be by someone who is not a party to the divorce. He or she must confirm the service by making a sworn statement (an affidavit) that the proper person received the documents. In some provinces and territories the person served is asked to sign an Acknowledgment of Service.

Spouse

One of two people who live in a marriage-like relationship, meaning the people co-habit and have a sexual component to the relationship. Traditionally, this has been defined as a man and a woman, but now some provinces and territories include common-law and same-sex relationships in the definition of spouse.

Substitutional service

Service of court documents on a party by a method other than by personally handing over the documents. This type of service may be by a notice in a newspaper or on a bulletin board at the court house advising the person that a court proceeding has been started. Alternatively, the court may order that the person be served by handing the documents to an adult who lives at the same address. Or the court may allow the documents to be sent by registered mail to the last known address.

Superior Court

The higher court in the province or territory that falls between the provincial court and the Court of Appeal. Some provinces and territories call it Supreme Court, as in the Supreme Court of British Columbia. Other provinces call it Queen's Bench, as in the Court of Queen's Bench. These courts can hear family and divorce applications.

Tracing service (also known as skip-tracing)

When you don't know where your spouse can be found for the purpose of serving him or her with the divorce court application, and asking relatives and friends has not produced results, you can use a tracing service.

These services can be found under "tracing" in the *Yellow Pages*. The service will look for your spouse in government and credit bureau databases. The fee is usually between $125 and $400 if your spouse is in Canada. The tracing service may or may not be able to help if your spouse is in another country.

Divorce Kits
Available for Download

All the forms you need to do your own divorce in your province or territory, complete with instructions and samples, can be purchased by download from <www.self-counsel.com>.

Alberta

Statement of Claim for Divorce

Affidavit of Service

Notice to Disclose

Notice of Mandatory Seminar

Request for Divorce (Without Oral Hearing)

Praecipe to Note in Default

Affidavit of Applicant

Child Support Data Sheets

Undue Hardship Claims

Request for Certificate of Divorce

Divorce Judgment without Oral Evidence

Divorce Judgment and Corollary Relief Order

Divorce Judgment without Oral Evidence (Edmonton)

Divorce Judgment and Corollary Relief Order (Edmonton)

British Columbia

Joint

Writ of Summons

Statement of Claim

Praecipe (Divorce Order)

Backing Sheet for Writ & Statement of Claim

Affidavit of Husband

Affidavit of Wife

Draft Order (Divorce Only)

Draft Order

Financial Statement

Registrar's Certificate of Pleadings

Praecipe (Certificate of Divorce)

Certificate of Divorce

Child Support Fact Sheet

Agreement as to Annual Income and Amount of Child Support

Supplementary Child Support Fact Sheets:

Special or Extraordinary Expenses

Shared Custody

Split Custody

Child 19 Years or Older

Undue Hardship

Income over $150 000

Sole

Writ of Summons

Statement of Claim

Backing sheet for Writ & Statement of Claim

Affidavit of Service

Praecipe (Requesting Search)

Praecipe (Divorce Order)

Certificate of Pleadings

Affidavit of Applicant

Draft Order (Divorce Only)
Draft Order
Financial Statement
Praecipe (Certificate of Divorce)
Certificate of Divorce
Child Support Fact Sheet
Agreement as to Annual Income and
    Amount of Child Support
Supplementary Child Support Fact Sheets:
    Special or Extraordinary Expenses
    Shared Custody
    Split Custody
    Child 19 Years or Older
    Undue Hardship
    Income over $150,000

Newfoundland & Labrador
Petition
Notice of Petition
Acknowledgment of Service
Notice of Motion
Divorce Judgment
Judgment (Form 8)
Request (Form 9)
Certificate of Divorce
Financial Statement

New Brunswick
Joint
Petition for Divorce (Joint) 72B
Financial Statement 72J
Affidavit (Joint)
Cover page for Trial Record
Index for Trial Record
Certificate of Readiness 47B
Request for Divorce 72K

Sole
Petition for Divorce (Sole)
Financial Statement
Affidavit of Service
Affidavit of Service by Mail
Acknowledgement of Receipt Card
Affidavit (Sole)
Cover Page for Trial Record
Index for Trial Record
Certificate of Readiness
Request for Divorce

Nova Scotia
Joint
Personal Representation
Application and Intake
Petition for Divorce
Parenting Statement
Statement of Financial Information
Statement of Property
Application for Judgment
Divorce Judgment
Corollary Relief Judgment

Sole
Personal Representation
Application and Intake 70.05A
Petition for Divorce (Sole) 70.18A
Filing the Petition
Serving the Petition
Affidavit of Service of Petition for Divorce
Affidavit of Service (Other Documents)
Parenting Statement 70.08A
Statement of Financial Information 70.09A
Statement of Property 70.09B
Application for Judgment 70.23B

Divorce Judgment 70.23C
Corollary Relief Judgment 70.23D or E
Waiver of Answer and Time Limits
Notice to Disclose
Parent Education & Separation Education

Nunavut

Joint
Joint Petition for Divorce
Affidavit of the Applicant
Request for Divorce (without oral hearing)
Divorce Judgment (without oral evidence)
Corollary Relief Order
Financial Statement
Child Support Guidelines Information Sheet
Child Support Data Sheets
Request for a Certificate of Divorce

Sole
Petition for Divorce
Notice to Respondent
Affidavit of Service
Affidavit of the Applicant
Request for Divorce (without oral hearing)
Divorce Judgment (without oral evidence)
Corollary Relief Order
Financial Statement
Child Support Guidelines Information Sheet
Child Support Data Sheets
Request for a Certificate of Divorce

Northwest Territories

Joint
Petition for Divorce
Affidavit of the Applicant

Request for Divorce (without oral hearing)
Divorce Judgment (without oral evidence)
Corollary Relief Order
Financial Statement
Child Support Guidelines Information Sheet
Child Support Data Sheets
Request for a Certificate of Divorce

Sole
Petition for Divorce
Notice to Respondent
Affidavit of Service
Affidavit of the Applicant
Request for Divorce (without oral hearing)
Divorce Judgment (without oral evidence)
Corollary Relief Order
Financial Statement
Child Support Guidelines Information Sheet
Child Support Data Sheets
Request for a Certificate of Divorce

Ontario

Family Court Branch
General Application — Form 8
Application for Divorce — Form 8A
Financial Statement — Form 13
Acknowledgement of Service — Form 6
Affidavit of Service — Form 6B
Affidavit for Divorce — Form 36
Certificate of the Clerk — Form 36A
Divorce Order — Form 25A
Support Deduction Order
Support Deduction Order Information Form
Certificate of Divorce — Form 36B

Ontario **Superior Court of Justice**

Joint

Petition for Divorce (Joint)
Financial Statement
Waiver of Financial Statements
Case Information Statement
Joint Affidavit
Notice of Motion (Joint)
Support Deduction Order
Support Deduction Order Information Form
Motion Record
Divorce Judgment (Joint)
Affidavit (re: no appeal — Joint)
Certificate of Divorce
Divorce Certificate Mail Order Form
Record Card (Backing Sheet)
Sample Backing Sheet

Sole

Backing Sheet/Record Card
Petition for Divorce
Financial Statement
Notice to File Financial
Statement (Sole)
Waiver of Financial Statements
Case Information Statement
Filing the Petition
Family Information Sessions
Serving the Petition
Affidavit
Affidavit of Service
Affidavit of Service by Mail
Affidavit (re: no appeal)
Motion Record
Acknowledgment of Receipt Card
Requisition and Notice of Motion (Sole)

Support Deduction Order
Support Deduction Order Information Form
Divorce Judgment (Sole)
Certificate of Divorce
Divorce Certificate Mail Order Form

Prince Edward Island

Joint

Joint Petition for Divorce
Financial Statement
Waiver of Financial Statements
Director of Child Welfare's Notice of
    Intention to Investigate and Report
Affidavit on Motion for Judgment
Registrar's Certificate
Divorce Judgment
Certificate of Divorce
Backing Sheets

Sole

Petition for Divorce (Sole)
Financial Statement
Notice to File Financial Statement
Waiver of Financial Statements
Director of Child Welfare's Notice of
    Intention to Investigate and Report
Affidavit of Service
Acknowledgement of Service
Requisition to Note Default and Notice
    of Motion for Judgment
Petitioner's Affidavit on Motion for
    Judgment
Registrar's Certificate
Divorce Judgment
Certificate of Divorce
Backing sheet

Saskatchewan

Joint

Petition for Divorce

Application for Judgment

Affidavit of Petitioner

Financial Statement

Waiver of Financial and Property
Statements

Agreement as to Child Support

Child Support Information Sheet

Child Support Calculation

Draft Child Support Judgment

Draft Judgment

Certificate of Divorce

Sole

Petition for Divorce

Affidavit of Personal Service

Notice of Application for Judgment

Application for Judgment

Affidavit of Petitioner

Financial Statement

Waiver of Financial and Property
Statements

Agreement as to Child Support

Child Support Information Sheet

Notice to File Income Information

Child Support Calculation

Draft Child Support Judgment

Draft Judgment

Certificate of Divorce

Yukon

Petition for Divorce

Notice to Respondent and Person Named

Financial Statement

Affidavit of Service

Request for Notice

Request for Divorce without a Hearing

Affidavit

Divorce Judgment

Corollary Relief Order

Notice to Petitioner

Request for a Certificate of Divorce

Certificate of Divorce

Manitoba

Joint

Petition for Divorce

Financial Statement

Requisition (Family Proceedings)

Affidavit of Husband/Wife

Divorce Judgment

Judgment

Sole

Petition for Divorce

Financial Statement

Acknowledgement of Service

Affidavit of Service

Affidavit of Petitioner's Evidence

Requisition (Family Proceedings)

Divorce Judgment

Judgment